HORIZON

JANUARY, 1960 · VOLUME II, NUMBER 3

HORIZON
A Magazine of the Arts

JANUARY, 1960 • VOLUME II, NUMBER 3

PUBLISHER
James Parton

EDITOR
Joseph J. Thorndike, Jr.

MANAGING EDITOR
William Harlan Hale

ASSOCIATE EDITORS
Ralph Backlund
Robert Emmett Ginna

ASSISTANT EDITORS
Ada Pesin
Jane Wilson

EDITORIAL ASSISTANTS
Shirley Abbott, Caroline Backlund,
Alan Doré, Martha Thomson

COPY EDITOR
Mary Ann Pfeiffer
Assistant: Rebecca R. Barocas

ART DIRECTOR
Irwin Glusker
Assistant: Emma Landau

ADVISORY BOARD
Gilbert Highet, *Chairman*
Frederick Burkhardt   Oliver Jensen
Marshall B. Davidson   Jotham Johnson
Richard M. Ketchum

EUROPEAN CONSULTING EDITOR
J. H. Plumb
Christ's College, Cambridge

EUROPEAN BUREAU
Gertrudis Feliu, *Chief*
28 Quai du Louvre, Paris

CIRCULATION DIRECTOR
Richard V. Benson

HORIZON is published every two months by
American Horizon, Inc., a subsidiary of American
Heritage Publishing Co., Inc., 551 Fifth Avenue,
New York 17, N. Y.
    Single Copies: $3.95
Annual Subscriptions: $18.00 in the U.S. & Can.
                $19.00 elsewhere

Second-Class postage paid at New York, N.Y.

HORIZON welcomes contributions but can assume
no responsibility for such unsolicited material.

COVER: In Tahiti the musical words *Fatata te Miti* mean "by the sea." Paul Gauguin chose them as the title for the canvas of which this is a detail, and which he painted in 1892. In it one encounters the blazing color and golden-skinned people that make up the enduring vision of the South Seas held by generations of Western travelers. An article on the Dream of the South Seas begins on page 28, and is followed by a portfolio in gravure of some of Gauguin's greatest paintings of the area. *Fatata te Miti* is in the Chester Dale Collection at the National Gallery of Art in Washington, D.C.

FRONTISPIECE: The great god Vishnu rides out to conquer evil in a palanquin of rare delight. Indeed, no more exotic conveyance could have been devised for the Hindu Preserver of the Universe than these artistically wreathed bodies of Indian dancing girls. This nineteenth-century Indian folk painting probably comes from a local school of Delhi and derives from an early Persian tradition of arranging human forms in the shape of objects or animals.

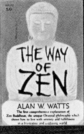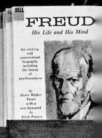
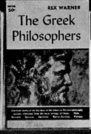
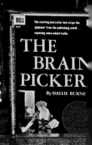

THE CULTURAL CLASS WAR

It is waged hot and heavy by the critics of Mass Culture
and the critics of Class Culture. Yet the co-existence of the two
forms quite often serves to enrich and enliven the arts in America

By ERIC LARRABEE

"Art happens—" said James McNeill Whistler, in one of his typically blunt pronouncements, "no hovel is safe from it, no Prince may depend on it, the vastest intelligence cannot bring it about, and puny efforts to make it universal end in quaint comedy, and coarse farce." Whistler had the advantage of being an artist and an egotist. He knew that most people care little for art as he understood it, and he asked only that they have the candor to admit as much. The question of what social system is best for art would have struck him as charming but absurd.

Today we are denied the alternative that Whistler's snobbery afforded him. To be a snob, at least publicly, is slightly disreputable, or at best irrelevant to the issues we think are important: What kind of society are we living in? Does America have a civilization, and, if so, is it of high or low quality? If the latter, what is wrong with us and how can it be changed? To all of these one might reply in Whistler's terms, but this would do little to answer the needs, or calm the anxieties, from which the questions arise.

Whatever it is we live in, it is widely known by the name of Mass Culture—that combination of industrialism, distributed authority, consumer goods, and increasing literacy and leisure, which first emerged in the United States and is now beginning to appear elsewhere. But we also (by "we" I mean educated, though not necessarily "officially" educated, Americans) live in a Class Culture—the complex of books and ideas, paintings and symphonies, judgments and

aspirations, that is our inheritance from the Western European past. The two are sometimes at odds, though neither could exist without the other. Both have sharply defined characteristics, though they are often found jumbled together in confusion, the vulgar and the esoteric cheek by jowl.

If I had to settle for a single image of the contemporary American culture, it would be an example of this diversity, like the paperback bookstore, with its row on row of titles cutting across a range of taste and quality so improbable that it can be described only in catch phrases: from the best seller to the out-of-print, from the sublime to the salacious, from the sensational to the sententious, from Aristotle to Zen.

American Class Culture has come a long distance in the forty-odd years since H. L. Mencken wrote "The Sahara of the Bozart," and denounced the entire South for being a cultural desert which could now no more produce a Washington or a Lee than Nicaragua could produce Aldous Huxley. "In all that gargantuan paradise of the fourth-rate," he wrote, in fine Menckenian fettle, "there is not a single picture gallery worth going into, or a single orchestra capable of playing the nine symphonies of Beethoven. . . ."

What of the South today? As for symphony orchestras, there are sixty-eight of them: twelve in Texas; ten in Florida; seven in North Carolina; six each in Missouri and Tennessee; five in Virginia; four each in South Carolina, Arkansas, and Alabama; three each in West Virginia and Louisiana; two in Georgia; and one each in Kentucky and Missis-

The new world of the paperbacks brings opposites together

sippi. There are museums by the score, and one of them (in Richmond) has an enormous air-conditioned van for carrying exhibits to less favored communities. Texas has given us Van Cliburn; and even Bob Jones University, Billy Graham's fundamentalist alma mater, is offering courses in Shakespeare and Biblical archaeology.

Mass Culture has made this happen, creating the abundant atmosphere in which Class Culture is enabled to flourish, along with everything else. The gain may be dubious, for the price we pay for it is an equal or greater flourishing of the cheap and ugly—the landscape along the American highways, the worst of the fare provided by the media, all the indulgence of vulgar and simple-minded appetites that would have sent Mencken into paroxysms of mirth and confirmed him in his low opinion of the American public. But it is too late now to back out. The two cultures are too entangled with one another to hope of pulling them apart; and the question is not whether they will have to live together, but how they can manage to get along.

The word "culture," in the two phrases, carries a heavy

Critics: tearful . . .

There is slowly emerging a tepid, flaccid Middlebrow Culture that threatens to engulf everything in its spreading ooze. Bauhaus modernism has at last trickled down, in a debased form of course, into our furniture, cafeterias, movie theaters, electric toasters, office buildings, drug stores, and railroad trains. . . . T. S. Eliot writes The Cocktail Party and it becomes a Broadway hit. . . . All this is not a raising of the level of Mass Culture, as might appear at first, but rather a corruption of High Culture. There is nothing more vulgar than sophisticated kitsch.
Dwight Macdonald, *A Theory of Mass Culture* 1953

load. Increasingly we use it in the anthropologist's sense (or a variation thereof) to mean the social milieu, the sum of the customs and ways of thinking in which the individual is reared, almost as a synonym for "society." At the same time, it has an overlapping implication from the word "cultured," with all its connotations of desirable though artificial refinement. In this respect we are not quite so self-conscious as the Soviet Union, where *nyekulturny* ("uncultured") can apparently signify any source of local shame, from "no sidewalks" to "without plumbing." But we are no less accustomed to thinking of "culture" as something that comes from the outside (from Europe, then from the urban Northeast), so that we are perennially vulnerable to the charge that everything good in our Class Culture is imported and imitative, while everything bad in our Mass Culture is truly and inimitably our own.

Asked what he had liked at an international music festival, a Parisian critic said, "The four Americans—Munch, Monteux, Balanchine, and Stravinsky." We lay ourselves open to that gibe whenever we try to show off our Class Culture. No matter how successfully we measure up to the traditional

standards, we can always be dismissed at the last moment with the bland observation that our performance is unauthentic. Are California wines admirable? Unfortunately they aren't French. Do people flock to our museums? Where did their collections come from? Do we produce first-rate piano players? Why can't we recognize them until someone else does it for us? Van Cliburn was playing Tchaikovsky and Rachmaninoff with fire and dexterity before he went to Moscow, but he returned a folk hero. They approved of him, and "they," being non-American, must know better than we.

We not only have an inferiority complex, we have a complex about the complex. We are ashamed of our shame. Americans who have undergone the hazing process of higher education are especially accessible to being reproached for, and told atrocity stories about, the generally low level of public taste. Our culture is a Mass Culture, and "Mass culture," as Dwight Macdonald succinctly puts it, "is not and never can be any good." This is the opinion of it which commonly prevails in educated American circles: that it is made up of gimcrack stuff; that it casts a pall of mediocrity over the rest of us; that it diverts the artist from his true purpose; that it saturates the society with appetizing irrelevancies; that it rots democracy, corrupts taste, defeats education, subverts the true and beautiful, and ought, in short, to be prohibited by Act of Congress.

This sleazy side of the Mass Culture society has for some reason a snakelike fascination for highbrows; they can't stand it, but they can't turn their eyes away. The last place on earth one would have expected a man of such fastidious taste as Aldous Huxley to live was Los Angeles, which might be called the Mother Lode of Mass Culture, but there indeed he lived for many years—in the very center of awfulness, which he himself called "the City of Dreadful Joy," with its revivalist sects, its happy cemeteries, its lunatic movie industry, its cult of healthy, sun-bronzed idiocy: from Muscle Beach at Santa Monica to the annual teen-age celebration of the vernal equinox at Balboa. This is what Mass Culture most often means to the highbrow—the quintessence of all the stuffed dolls, jukeboxes, outlandish architecture, scatological post cards, comic books, roadside pottery stands, adenoidal singers with duck-tailed haircuts there ever were or will be—and he lavishes on it his most scornful rhetoric.

There is no useful argument here. Certainly no one will leap to defend the national genius in terms of these unhappy expressions of it, and as a result anyone who plays them as trump cards will win his trick. Scoring points off Mass Culture makes for an innocent sport, and the Mass Culture itself obligingly behaves badly enough to justify the worst of its critics' assertions. Even one of the most sympathetic of them, Gilbert Seldes, was led in a moment of disenchantment to invent the Seldes, or Sewer, Theory of Mass Culture, according to which no popular art reaches its peak until a new one arrives to drain off its superfluous personnel: the theater didn't amount to anything until movies came along, movies didn't

6

amount to anything until radio came along, radio didn't amount to anything until television came along, and so on.

More power to the critics, then. But there has to be a distinction made between criticizing the products of Mass Culture and damning it for its very existence. The people who really do not like it at all, such as Dwight Macdonald, move rather deftly from one to the other, so that you are still admiring their witty vivisection of some popular idol when you discover that the commercial has started. The critics of Mass Culture in this category—they would include Macdonald, Clement Greenberg, Ernest van den Haag, Irving Howe, William Phillips, many of them contributors to *Partisan Review* or to *Mass Culture,* the most comprehensive anthology on the subject—are not satisfied simply to demolish its manifestations; they are against it on principle, and the principle is the real seat of the debate.

I think it would not be unfair to summarize their position somewhat as follows: the creating and preserving of High (or Class) Culture has always been the concern of, at most, a small minority, an elite with both leisure and long practice in the exercise of refined discrimination. Any attempt to share this culture with a larger group results only in diluting it and distracting the elite from its proper job of defending and conserving High Art. Mass Culture, from this perspective, is a perpetual threat to Class Culture. Mass Culture is fundamentally inimical to elites of all kinds; it lowers the level of potential appreciation by exposing young people to a steady diet of trash; and it undermines the artist, last but not least, by presenting him with endless opportunities to sell out. It breathes an air of poisonously attractive fog, in which High Art cannot thrive.

To the highbrow, the worst enemy is not the lowbrow but the middlebrow. First of all, the highbrow has always had a mellow affection for what he imagines to have been the folk cultures of the past, in which kings and peasant-poets acknowledged their need for one another. Lowbrow culture does not threaten him, if indeed it knows that he exists. Secondly, just as a fanatic believer feels more menaced by the moderates of his own faith than by the enemy, so the partisans of High Culture see the most danger in those who presume to popularize it—the editors, book reviewers, captive intellectuals of the media, and all the other camouflaged Philistines who masquerade as allies of High Art but at heart are not. Surrounded by the swamp of middlebrow culture, the fortress of quality must hold out to the last, above all against the danger that the swamp will become attractive to the defenders and tempt them to abandon the citadel in search of chimerical, momentary gains.

For the artist, the Class Culturists ask not only the right but the duty to be "alienated" from society. They maintain that nothing else will nourish him, that many a great artist in the past has been to some degree at odds with his time, and that his best work has either been strengthened by this antipathy or defaced by its absence. They are continually doing battle against the demand (which William James made, to no avail, on his brother Henry) that the artist should be vigorous, affirmative, and hence more "American." Critics like Bernard DeVoto, John Chamberlain, Allan Nevins, J. Donald Adams, and Gerald W. Johnson have for years been urging novelists to contend more ardently with the "realities" of American life, especially the life of business enterprise; but the observable result has been only a shelfful of rather shallow works, while the writers of greater skill have persisted in cultivating the rank and curious growths in their private corner of the garden.

To the artist in search of alienation, the most deplorable of all societies is a cheerful, positive, forward-looking one like ours, which determinedly seeks every day to become more admirable in every way, including many that serve the artist's own convenience and comfort. To his most slashing and vicious cries of outrage it replies, "Yes, you're so right," and offers him a contract for a schedule of appearances on TV programs with Mike Wallace or David Susskind. There is something both brave and saddening in the extreme

... and cheerful

Nevertheless there remains plenty of respectable cultural activity, plenty of opportunity for devotees of the most unpopular kinds of beauty and truth. The pure sciences are clearly prosperous as never before; there appear to be easy chairs enough for historians, philosophers, and scholars generally; there is no dearth even of fine art. . . . Artists and thinkers today need make no sacrifice of integrity, and the best of them have made none. I doubt that any genius, or many robust, first-rate talents, have been either frustrated or devoured by the masses.

Herbert J. Muller, *Science and Criticism* 1956

measures the Beat have therefore had to adopt in order to get out from under this blanket of sympathetic understanding by their elders. What they envy in the earlier generations is a visible enemy. "I would propose," as the novelist Norman Mailer has written, "that the artist feels most alienated when he loses the sharp sense of what he is alienated from. . . . Today, the enemy is vague, the work seems done, the audience more sophisticated than the writer."

Here is where I part company with my friend and classmate, Mr. Mailer. He is asking, not that the world measure up to his demands as an artist—which are considerable, as they deserve to be, but that it satisfy his preconception of how an artist ought to behave. This knowledge comes from the recorded careers of artists for the past few centuries; it comes, that is, from books, and it smells, if I may use an old-fashioned expression, of the lamp. Are the standards of Class Culture so arbitrary as to define the everyday world as beneath our interest? Are we bound by a previous generation's experience to seek either similar experiences or none at all? Are my requirements for alienation determined by what happened to a half-dozen people in Paris in 1923?

TEXT CONTINUED ON PAGE 10

7

	MOVIES	CHAIRS	RESORTS	THE DANCE
STRICTLY FOR THE MASS These are aimed at crowd instincts as some see them	"The Return of the Fly," 1959	BarcaLounger reclining chair	Fireworks at Palisades Park, N. J.	Rockettes, Radio City Music Hall
PRETENSIONS TO CLASS These cater to that yearning for finer things	"War and Peace" in Technicolor	Executive chair by Charles Eames	White Sulphur Springs' Greenbrier	"Art" dance of faun and nymph
UP FROM THE MASS Where the vernacular produces unexpected art	Charlie Chaplin's "Shoulder Arms"	Old ice-cream parlor type	Disneyland, Calif.	Jitterbug contest, St. Louis
GENUINE CLASS Proving the far-flung response to real quality	Paddy Chayevsky's "Marty"	Sling or butterfly chair	Music festival at Tanglewood	Scene from "West Side Story"

Mass and Class on the American Grid

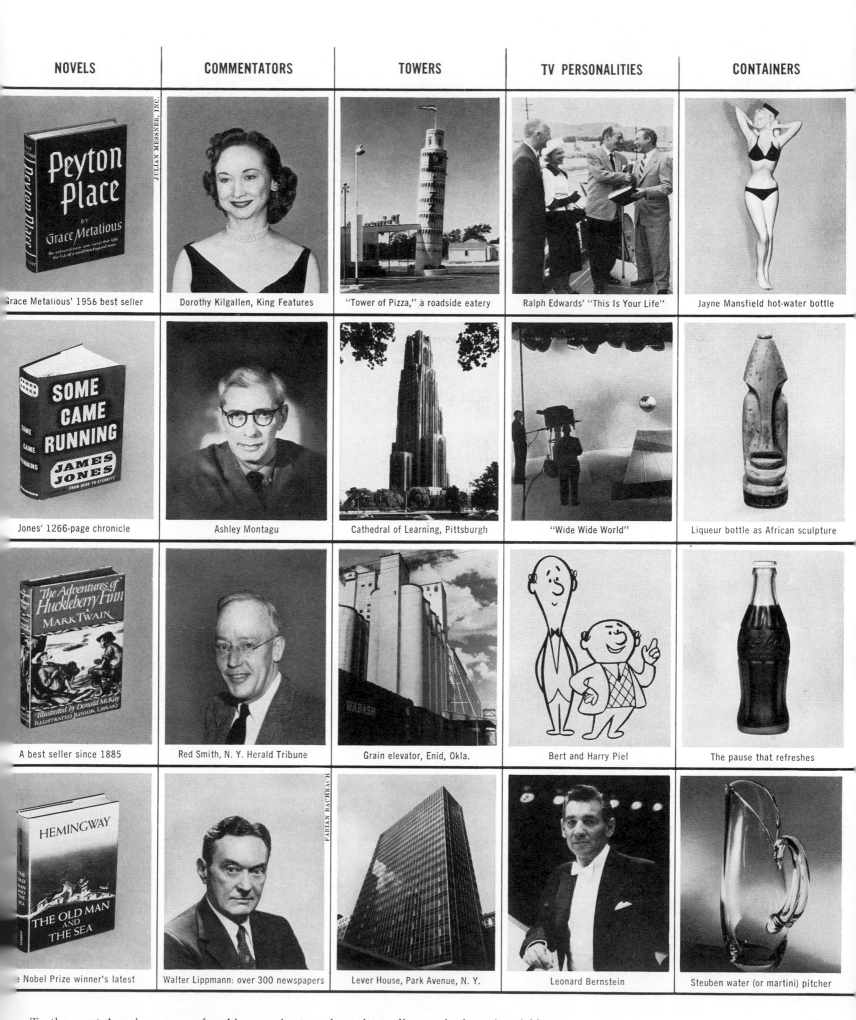

NOVELS	COMMENTATORS	TOWERS	TV PERSONALITIES	CONTAINERS
Grace Metalious' 1956 best seller	Dorothy Kilgallen, King Features	"Tower of Pizza," a roadside eatery	Ralph Edwards' "This Is Your Life"	Jayne Mansfield hot-water bottle
Jones' 1266-page chronicle	Ashley Montagu	Cathedral of Learning, Pittsburgh	"Wide Wide World"	Liqueur bottle as African sculpture
A best seller since 1885	Red Smith, N. Y. Herald Tribune	Grain elevator, Enid, Okla.	Bert and Harry Piel	The pause that refreshes
The Nobel Prize winner's latest	Walter Lippmann: over 300 newspapers	Lever House, Park Avenue, N. Y.	Leonard Bernstein	Steuben water (or martini) pitcher

To the great American game of making up charts and graphs to diagram both one's neighbors and one's self, HORIZON adds this variant of its own as a gloss to the article by Eric Larrabee that precedes it. It groups an assortment of cultural and social manifestations in America's midst today according to four categories of intention and achievement. The game can of course be played differently with other categories, or pursued indefinitely with other choices.

Mozart in one night produced the Overture to Don Giovanni. *These forty people (plus twenty more) labored three weeks to produce a 60-second commercial for an anti-halitosis tablet.*

TEXT CONTINUED FROM PAGE 7

Mass Culture too has its partisans. There are not many of them hardy enough to be found on the barricades where the attack is fiercest, willing to defend a Coca-Cola bottle against Greek vases or Erskine Caldwell against Dante. But they have something to say on this score, nonetheless. It would begin, I think, with the rather obvious assertion that "culture" is not a set of objects and abstractions. It does not belong to anybody in particular, and it cannot be handed around like a plate of candy. It is a process. It is our effort to make a significant pattern, in sounds or colors or words, out of our fugitive and chaotic sense impressions. "Culture" is the attempt; "art" is the infrequent, the ever-to-be-hoped-for success. Logan Pearsall Smith, who like Whistler had the advantage of being a snob, put it elegantly: "The indefatigable pursuit of an unattainable Perfection, even though it consist in nothing more than in the pounding of an old piano, is what alone gives meaning to our life on this unavailing star."

The lesson of Mass Culture is in Smith's clause about the piano. It is possible, on an old piano, to achieve art; it is also possible, with an entire symphony orchestra and an audience in full evening dress, to achieve nothing but banality. Class Culture, too, has its vices, and one of them is the inability to protect standards without also protecting those who merely give the standards lip service. Many are the efforts now being made to maintain standards, as Admiral Rickover wants us to do for the sake of the Cold War and Jacques Barzun for the sake of Culture. But I find nothing in their remedies that promises us any better protection than we *have* against the mechanical rabbits, the plausible manipulators of received ideas who go through all the motions of High Culture but have forgotten, if they ever knew, what it is all about. The man at the old piano, whether Beethoven or Jelly Roll Morton, is the one who remembers.

The study of Mass (or "Popular") Culture is necessarily the study of as many kinds of artistic expression as possible, from the most formal to the most casual, from the trivial to the portentous. It requires that architecture, city planning, the design of tools and machinery, the popular press, colloquial speech, folk songs and folk tales all be given as much and as serious attention as statues, sonnets, and sonatas. It is, moreover, a relatively new endeavor. Two of its most adventurous American pioneers, Gilbert Seldes and Lewis Mumford, are still among its most vigorous practitioners. But it has been started, and sturdily enough so that the arbitrary line between High Culture and Low, in terms of what a scholar may properly examine, can no longer be maintained.

The broadening of critical perspective to include Mass Culture can also have a potentially beneficial effect on Class Culture, for it raises the continual test of relevance. Works of art which are fragmentary, untutored, or spontaneously generated by day-to-day existence show the culture-process working much closer to the surface, so to speak; they serve as an ever-present reminder that art is either anchored in life or eventually loses its power. Just as a gourmet now and then prefers a plain omelet or potato soup, to remind him what food was originally for, so even the most sophisticated listener will now and then turn to folk music, to remind himself that without emotion there would be no music at all. The tingling at the nerve ends is the same, whether it is Isobel Baillie singing "I Know That My Redeemer Liveth" from Handel's *Messiah*, or Mahalia Jackson singing "I'm Goin' to Move on up a Little Higher," and in this respect whether one is "as good as" the other is beside the point.

Yet jazz, the motion picture, and journalism—to name the three most promising of the popular arts—have all had to live through a tedious and unnecessarily prolonged denial of their credentials as "serious." Should Bach Be Swung? Can Marilyn *Really* Act? Should a Writer Write for Money? There have turned out to be endless inventions for evading the only essential issue, which is that every craft must be judged in its own terms, and not those of some other craft. A movie is not a photographed stage play, a jazz composition is not a classical composition that didn't quite make it, and a journalist is not an academic scholar gone wrong. To their credit, the popular arts have one quality in common: they will not be patronized. When you try to film an opera merely by performing it in front of a camera, the result is a monstrosity like the movie *Tales of Hoffmann*. When an academic writer attempts to engage in what he calls "popularization," the result often shows only that he despises what he is doing. When José Iturbi tried to play boogiewoogie, the result was one of the worst recordings ever heard.

The emergence of Mass Culture has emphasized what should have been obvious all along: that there can be no distinction between the good and bad in art on the basis of medium or subject matter. *Don Giovanni* was popular art when it was first performed, and apparently the first-night audience in Prague liked it a lot better than it was liked for many years thereafter by listeners who should have been better prepared for it. Even the artist's immediate motive is immaterial. Masterpieces have been written, painted, and composed for cash or, even worse, for favor—the faint, sniveling expectation of cash to come. Men of the greatest genius, like Mozart, have had to perform prodigies of obsequiousness simply in order to eat, and then have produced, practically on demand, works of unparalleled freshness and originality.

What matters is not who pays the artist but whether or not he is Mozart, and that is something we are not lucky enough to be able to ask more than once or twice every few centuries. At least Mass Culture would have treated him better than Class Culture did. I do not know how "alienated" Mozart felt it necessary to be, but I rather imagine him (if alive today) doing a Broadway show every few years, a commission or two from the Louisville Symphony, and in between, a steady schedule of concert tours—in short, a life very much like that of Leonard Bernstein. Perhaps it will be argued that civilization would then be the loser, since without the threat of starvation hanging over him Mozart might not have turned out that incredible stream of music in his brief lifetime—just as Dr. Obispo, a character in Aldous Huxley's *After Many a Summer,* remarks that he could have cured Keats's vitamin B deficiency and saved the world a lot of unnecessary poetry. There is more here than a joke, but if that is the choice we have to make, I will vote for peace, good health, and fair weather—and against killing off Mozart of Bright's disease at the age of thirty-five.

There are some other things to be said for Mass Culture, several of which I have put off saying because they are so obvious, but perhaps there are one or two unobvious sides to them. First of all, as a debating point, should have come *availability*—the utterly unprecedented availability of the paperback book or the long-playing record—since this is everywhere evident and everywhere praised. It is difficult enough to find adequate words to describe this revolution, which has put whole libraries of literature and music within the general reach, let alone to define the differences it has already made in our attitudes and assumptions. One way of picturing it, and of bowing once more to the shade of Mozart, is to point out that anyone with access to a well-stocked record-lending library can now listen to the major portion of his fantastic output—nearly all of the symphonies, all of the string quartets, many of the violin sonatas, all of the piano sonatas, all of the piano concertos (and most of them for other instruments), most of the serenades and *divertimenti,* much of the choral music, and many more of the operas than used to be regularly performed. We can now, in other words, hear most of Mozart, something only the most assiduous concertgoer, a generation ago, could have hoped to do.

A common failing of abundance is to take itself for granted. It is just as easy to buy a paperback, and not read

it, as a hard-cover book; and we are properly chagrined at our easygoing indifference when something occurs like Leonard Bernstein's tour with the New York Philharmonic behind the Iron Curtain. The good will shown is in itself not unusual, though very gratifying, but the riots in the ticket lines, the forty-minute ovations, the crowds filling the streets afterward—these would be inconceivable in the United States. Do we value the Philharmonic the less, or are we merely used to it? Have these foreign audiences been on such a meager musical diet, or have our appetites gone jaded? At any event, here are people starved for what we have in plenty.

But the terrible beauty of abundance is that it makes us choose. If to some degree we are prisoners of our indifference, the Polish and Russian audiences are similarly prisoners of their hunger. The choice may be tacit, a sin of omission, but it cannot be passed off as required by circumstances beyond our control. Availability does away with the other excuses. The book that sits there, actually on the shelf, cries out to be read, and if you cannot read it, perhaps the reason is that you find it dull; the moment may come when you can admit to yourself that you find Stendhal dull, or Henry Adams, or whoever, and here is the beginning of wisdom.

Availability also, in a paradoxical way, puts a premium on quality. Nothing is better calculated to separate the second- and third-rate from the best than continual exposure, and one more effect of Mass Culture on Class Culture is to subject the most sacred masterpieces to the test of actually being read, and seen, and listened to. Much music cannot stand to be heard in the home, where it must compete continually with the distractions of family, mobility, and household noise. A composition that seemed impressive, when you were stuck to your seat in the reverential hush of the concert hall, may now reveal itself as a mass of heaving and billowing noise, calculated mainly to impress the already impressed.

Class Culture, in a Mass Culture society, is thus reduced to its essential strengths, and it has the unequaled advantage of being cheap. It is by far the least expensive of modern leisure activities, and it has the further virtue of being inexhaustible—the only condition is that you really care. If you really care about what is in books and paintings, there will be more than enough of them for you—and enough within them—to last at least this lifetime. The only condition is that you confront your own need for Art, and find it genuine. Abundance asks only that you choose. The twentieth century has no doubt more than enough in it that is worth ignoring, but it is the only century we are going to get. Time passes; eras have each their weaknesses and strengths; and the only divine purpose evident in history— as Robert Frost once said—is that it shall always be equally difficult for a man to save his soul.

This is the second in a series of inquiries by Mr. Larrabee into America's social order today. The first, "The Wreck of the Status System," appeared in the November, 1959, HORIZON.

NEW LIFE

America has produced no Mozart, Verdi, or Puccini. Yet it is the

To judge by the repertory of masterpieces that are performed year in and year out in the world's great opera houses—and I can think of no better way of judging—opera, in the twentieth century, has undergone an unprecedented decline. Only a handful of operatic works of this century have managed to hold the boards or to gain any firm grip on the affections of the public, and most of these are the productions of two composers, Richard Strauss and Giacomo Puccini, both with strong roots in the nineteenth century, and both now dead. This does not mean that composers have ceased writing operas. Indeed, the number of operas written since 1900 is probably as great as that produced in any period of musical history. But most modern works in the form, including such celebrated ones as Alban Berg's *Wozzeck*, Stravinsky's *The Rake's Progress,* and the efforts of the British composers Benjamin Britten and William Walton, have turned out to be flawed affairs—musicodramatic experiments which lack the elements that draw and retain the enthusiasm of confirmed operagoers.

The principal element lacking is the creation of dramatic tension by means of melodies that are really worth singing—that make demands on, and exploit, the expressive power of great voices. This element is, and always has been, the basic feature of operatic craftsmanship. You can view an opera as a drama (a large number of them are strong ones), or you can shut your eyes and think of an opera as a purely musical experience (and some of them are fine musical experiences).

But neither of these attitudes covers the operatic experience completely. Some operas are better dramas than others; some are musically more interesting. Few are perfect works of art. But one thing all good operas have in common is that they are meant to be sung by voices of unusual caliber.

It is this that sets opera apart from the spoken drama, the musical show, and the art of symphonic music. If you don't like fine song, you don't like opera, and it is mainly the loss among composers of the capacity to create fine song that has landed opera in its present predicament. Curiously, the predicament does not affect either the art of opera singing, which still holds to a high level of quality, or the popularity of opera in the grand old-fashioned manner, which continues to draw audiences, and, in fact, draws them in greater numbers than ever before. The weakness has been exclusively that of the modern operatic composer, who has been deprived of his traditions by at least a generation of muddleheaded thinking as to what opera is all about, and thus left fiddling with all manner of superficial technical tricks, none of which constitutes the trick of writing effectively for the voice.

Of all the operatic works of this comparatively barren period, Berg's *Wozzeck* stands out as perhaps the most interesting and certainly as one of the most representative. Many people find its libretto—a play written by the precocious early nineteenth-century German dramatist Georg Büchner—a moving thing, despite its dated air of social protest and its grisly, hopeless concentration-camp atmosphere.

By WINTHROP SARGEANT

IN THE OLD OPERA HOUSE

seat of a revival of a long neglected form in the hands of spirited contemporaries

Its orchestral fabric is extremely complicated, and contains a few flashes of real genius, as well as some long passages of pedantically rigid atonal writing. It is amusing to note that *Wozzeck* contains one unadorned major, or do-mi-sol, chord which Berg wrote at a point where the hero is discussing money. Berg himself stated that he considered it a commonplace chord, and that he used it deliberately to convey the commonplace character of this medium of exchange. The implication, of course, is that all opera written prior to Berg's time—all of it rich in major chords of this sort—is commonplace, a position that could be assumed only by a cultural parvenu.

Still, *Wozzeck* is an engrossing melodrama with music that is technically interesting. The trouble with it as an opera lies in its treatment of the human voice, which is used not for singing but for the sort of declamation (ranging from groans to screeches) known as *Sprechgesang*, or "speech song." This type of declamation is not only unlovely, it begs the whole operatic question. It does not require, or exploit, the singing voice. Properly speaking, *Wozzeck* is not an opera at all, or perhaps one should describe it as an opera for people who don't like opera. Like most of the works of its era, it seems bent on demolishing the very thing people go to opera houses to hear. It marks not the beginning of a new operatic style, but the destructive finish of a great tradition—a finish in which gleams of past genius become buried in grotesquerie, mannerism, and technical complexity used as an end in itself.

A cynic might simply write off opera as one of the great art forms of the past, like the Greek or Elizabethan drama, and conclude that it has had its day. But several factors tend to undermine this hasty view. For one thing, to singers and audiences opera is very much alive. For another, there has, very recently, been considerable evidence of a revival of interest in good opera on the part of some contemporary composers. The traditions of the art are being restudied. The clutter of bad, unsingable opera that marred the first half of the century is beginning to be forgotten. Composers here and there, like the gifted Frenchman Francis Poulenc, are abandoning the decadent mannerisms of the period between the two world wars and are writing singable melody again. It is perhaps too early to speak of this rather tentative movement as a renaissance. But it does show a reawakening on the part of composers to the infinite possibilities of the human voice as a vehicle for dramatic expression, and a wish to compete again with the acknowledged masters of an art that has been carried on ever since the seventeenth century.

The most interesting feature of this movement—perhaps because it is the most unexpected—is the sudden appearance of a lively school of American opera composers, whose works are appealing to fairly large audiences in a nation that heretofore has never been considered a stronghold of operatic composition. The best of the new American operas may not be masterpieces. But one might reflect, in this connection, that even the golden age of eighteenth- and nineteenth-century

13

opera saw hundreds of flops for each deathless contribution to the repertory. The important fact, I think, which suggests that a valid new operatic tradition is taking shape in this country, is that audiences in America are now going to performances of American opera, not out of a sense of cultural duty or a grim crusading effort at artistic snobbery, but simply to enjoy the combination of song, orchestral music, and drama as the engaging thing it ought to be. In a period in which symphonic composition has become largely a moribund exercise in academic techniques, this new sprouting of the operatic art has a special freshness and immediacy of appeal. Potentially it seems to me the most exciting thing that has happened in the history of American highbrow music.

The movement seems to have started at least two decades ago with the first operatic compositions of the Italo-American Gian-Carlo Menotti, who set himself in opposition to the dissonant formulas of what was then known as "modern music." Hooking himself to the tradition of Puccini, he succeeded in turning out a series of melodious works that attained considerable public recognition both at the Metropolitan Opera House and on Broadway. And although he has betrayed certain weaknesses now and then as a musical dramatist, he remains the movement's most successful pioneer. Since his first efforts, which were emphatically deplored by the doctrinaire crusaders for rigid unpleasantness in contemporary music—and emphatically enjoyed by the public which had no aesthetic axes to grind—a whole group of other composers has emerged, dedicated to good melody and effective drama and bent on resuscitating opera from the dark age imposed upon it by the Weimar Republic, the Parisian school known as *Les Six,* the Stravinskyites, and the Viennese atonalists. The new American school has been modest in its aims and simple and lucid in its writing. It still retains these characteristics.

Two and a half years ago the Ford Foundation looked over the field and decided to give it a boost by financing a spring festival of American opera at the New York City Center of Music and Drama. This undertaking has recently been followed by a move of nationwide scope—a grant by the Ford Foundation of nearly a million dollars to the Metropolitan, the New York City Opera, and the opera houses of Chicago and San Francisco to assist them in commissioning and presenting eighteen new American operas. The first festival was a definite success. It proved the existence of an American school of operatic composition and brought together, for comparison, a number of its most representative works. The public liked most of them, liked the idea of American opera, and came back next year for more. Meanwhile, this shot in the arm encouraged composers all over the country to try their hand at opera; and the New York City Opera, which had been the producing organization for the Ford Foundation's venture, was swamped with manuscripts.

Many composers, tired of the formulas from which "abstract" music is now suffering, saw a ray of light in the "concrete" emotional sort of music that good opera calls for. It is,

Kurt Weill   *Douglas Moore*   *Samuel Barber*

at the moment, impossible to estimate the result of this artistic migration. The Ford Foundation and Julius Rudel, the general director of the New York City Opera, have been able to produce only a fraction of the output. They hope that the fraction they *have* produced is the best. The valiant and underpaid staff of the New York City Opera's singers, conductors, stage directors, and scenic designers, have performed miracles in mounting the chosen operas. The festival has become a labor of enthusiasm that has been rewarded with at least a few productions of lasting importance.

As one analyzes the best of these productions, seeking to find out the character of the new tradition they are evolving, one is struck by the directness and simplicity of their purpose. Nobody is trying to go Wagner and Strauss one better in the direction of complexity. Nobody is trying to save the world with an aesthetic revolution, or to create a type of musical drama the likes of which have never been seen before. The idea seems rather to latch onto a good play, or a good dramatic idea, and embellish it with music that enhances its emotional values and speaks to the heart of almost any reasonably sensitive listener. As this has been the idea behind most of the great operas of history, it seems an eminently sound one.

Probing a little further into the phenomenon of contemporary American opera, one is struck by the fact that its tradition has two main roots. One of these is the Broadway musical show, which, of course, has been a flourishing commercial enterprise as well as a pleasing and popular art form for many years; and which, in certain musically more ambitious works (for example, Jerome Kern's *Show Boat* and more recent productions such as *The Music Man* and *Most Happy Fella*), has approached opera in complexity.* This is a healthy root, and its growth into full-fledged opera demands only a somewhat more searching preoccupation with human psychology, continuous reliance on music instead of gags, and the addition of the sort of vocal requirements that provide challenges, both in technique and dramatic expressiveness, for singers of professional training and operatic caliber. The type of music written for Douglas Moore's *Ballad of Baby Doe* (one of the American Opera Festival's unquestioned hits), for example, does not differ much in general style from that written by Richard Rodgers for *Oklahoma!* Where *The Ballad of Baby Doe* does differ from *Oklahoma!* is in the greater subtlety of its musical workmanship, the greater strength of its drama, and the bigger vocal challenges it offers to its cast.

*See the article "From the Shapely Form to a New Art Form" in HORIZON for September, 1958.

Carlisle Floyd   *Vittorio Giannini*   *Gian-Carlo Menotti*

The other main root of the current American opera tradition is the age-old art of the Italian opera, the fountainhead of all operatic craftsmanship and an art which, though more elaborate than the art of the American musical show, is at bottom a simple union of drama with expressive and vocally demanding melody. It is no coincidence that most of the American exponents of this root are men of Italian ancestry (or, in the case of Menotti, of Italian birth) who have found in their ancestral heritage a time-tried method that can be applied to thoroughly modern works. Besides Menotti, these Italo-American opera composers now include a number of particularly bright and skillful musical dramatists, among them Vittorio Giannini, Norman dello Joio, Marc Bucci, and Dominick Argento. These men seem to be restoring the Italian opera tradition in contemporary American form, with librettos written in English, and, at the moment at least, appear to be outdistancing anything that is being done in Italy.

It is idle to speculate whether the two roots will fuse, and such a fusion is probably not even desirable. The fact is that American operas with affinities to the musical show and American operas descended from the Italian tradition are equally effective. Each of them speaks a musical language intelligible to the operatic audience. Each is grounded solidly in a valid musical tradition. This last point is particularly important, for it was one of the cardinal faults of the bad opera of the early twentieth century that its composers imagined they could throw tradition overboard, and hence succeeded only in mystifying, instead of communicating with, their audiences.

Thus, the contemporary school of American opera is generally dedicated to arousing communicative interest. The play, the melodies, and the vocal hurdles are now the thing; the composer uses only such technical virtuosity as contributes to the effectiveness of the result. People who are in the habit of immersing themselves in the complexities of Wagner or Debussy, or in the modernistic twelve-tone system of composition known as atonality, will find the result deceptively simple, "popular" in melodic style, and perhaps even old-fashioned and conservative from the purely musical standpoint. But there is no denying that it is engaging to the unprejudiced listener and that it gives promise of a brilliant future.

Among the members of this new American school, certain individuals stand out as having made contributions of special quality. First let us consider Gian-Carlo Menotti, since he is both the most prolific and the most widely known composer of the group. Unlike the majority, he writes his own librettos and insists on personally directing most of his productions. He is the author of nearly a dozen works in the form, and has developed a sureness of technique in dealing with the musical stage that is probably unmatched by any of his contemporaries. He prefers Broadway to the Metropolitan Opera House, because Broadway productions permit him more leeway in dominating every detail of casting and staging; and, as opera composers go, he has enjoyed an enormous success there. The cultists of highbrow music have been irritated by this success and have criticized him for his unending facility, the comparatively popular and uncomplicated Italian character of his music, and the sure-fire clichés which sometimes invade his operatic ideas. To my mind, only the last criticism has any validity, and it does not by any means apply to all his operas. Menotti is facile, to be sure, but his facility involves tremendous skill in manipulating the mechanics of opera. He has an uncanny instinct for choosing the right English words to go with his musical settings, for writing graceful melodies to them, and for making the most of such dramatic situations as contribute to the purely operatic values of his stage spectacles. Sometimes these situations—as in *The Saint of Bleecker Street* and *Maria Golovin,* as well as in the libretto he wrote for Samuel Barber's *Vanessa*—seem to be stock ones derived from late nineteenth-century Italian opera, and are not particularly original. His dramas are not always strong ones. He has trouble with sharply defined characters: his heroines are apt to be somewhat ambiguous figures, and his heroes are often men of weak character, suffering from blindness, lameness, or mental derangement. These weaknesses apparently arise from Menotti's personal tragic outlook. They are complemented on the musical side by a penchant for light melodic invention which plays poetically around nostalgic and sometimes neurotic emotion, and very seldom attains real passion.

But these criticisms, at least as they concern drama, can also be made of many a contemporary playwright. On the other side, there are several impressive qualities in his work, including his mastery of orchestration, his deft, intuitive sense of effective spectacle, and his skill in writing for the voice.

To my mind *The Medium,* written in 1946, remains Menotti's most nearly perfect opera. Its dimensions do not strain his creative capacities. Its story is neat, compact, and highly original, dealing with an eerie, semi-supernatural situation, and it moves on toward its final melodramatic punch with a sense of the theater which is at once hair-raising and nostalgically tender. Nowhere else, so far, has he attained quite this degree of conciseness and formal coherence, although he has written several much more ambitious works. Of these, *The Island God* (a transitional work and a flop at the Metropolitan in 1942), *The Saint of Bleecker Street,* and *Maria Golovin* are conceived on the scale of grand opera and are unquestionably somewhat uneven in quality, though they contain some moving moments. The hero of *The Saint of Bleecker Street* is a weak-minded juvenile delinquent, and the hero of

TEXT CONTINUED ON PAGE 122

15

OVERLEAF: ORIGINAL DESIGNS FOR AMERICAN OPERAS

Donald Oenslager designed Douglas Moore's The Ballad of Baby Doe *(above) for its première at Central City, Colorado, in 1956. Jo Mielziner designed Kurt Weill's* Street Scene *(below) when Dwight Deere Wiman and the Playwrights Company offered it on Broadway in 1947. Both works were revived at the N. Y. City Center in 1958–1959.*

ORIGINAL DESIGNS FOR AMERICAN OPERAS

Grand operas of the nineteenth century were often set in grim castles, mountain caves, or the naves of soaring cathedrals: places appropriate to the romantic fervors of such men as Wagner and Verdi. Today's operas in America tend to be concerned with less full-blown, romantic themes and thus call for more mundane settings: a garish frontier hotel, the somber façade of a city brownstone, the shuttered drawing room of a twentieth-century neurotic. But the original sketches by four leading stage designers reproduced here suggest that even such themes may produce settings of sumptuous elegance or of haunting power.

Rouben Ter-Arutunian designed this set for Gian-Carlo Menotti's
Maria Golovin, *first performed at the Brussels World's Fair. It too*
was mounted at the N. Y. City Center, after failure on Broadway.

Cecil Beaton won applause for his settings for Vanessa, *composed*
by Samuel Barber to a libretto by Gian-Carlo Menotti and given
a highly successful première at the Metropolitan Opera in 1958.

By ALLAN TEMKO

LIFTING THE FEDERAL FACADE

If the U.S. Government can build such handsome embassies abroad, why can't it give the folks at home something better than Post-office Roman?

Since the founding of the Republic one of the paradoxes of American civilization has been its failure to create an adventurous public architecture worthy of a democratic state. In a nation consecrated to independence and progress and established in rebellion against Old World domination, Federal architecture—the architecture sponsored by Washington's officialdom—from its beginning has been characterized by imitation of the European past, as if this country had nothing to add to history. Over the generations copybook building has spread from Washington throughout the Union in a welter of pedimented post offices, colonnaded courthouses, turreted penitentiaries, ducal mints, and more recently, in pseudo-Modern but basically derivative Federal office buildings that supposedly are emblematic of progressive government. Yet after having put up with this situation for so long, today the public, and the Congress with it, have awakened to the implications of a sham Federal image. A revolution in Federal architecture is under way at last.

Yet, paradoxically, the revolution—still in its early stages—has thus far achieved its most striking successes not in the continental United States, but in distant places such as New Delhi, Kobe, Accra, and Oslo, where the State Department has embarked

Elegant, cheerful, and set in a garden, the new U. S. Consulate at Kobe (opposite) is one of many handsome modern buildings the government is erecting abroad. But at home we continue to settle for the debased and ponderous classicism exemplified in the recently completed Senate Office Building in Washington, D.C. (right).

19

T. S. SATYAN; COURTESY *Architectural Forum*

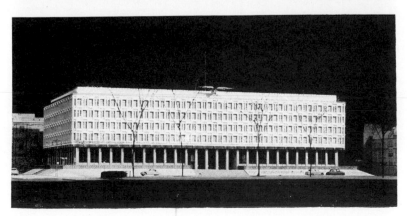

The most admired of the embassies built under the State Department's new program is the one at New Delhi (left), where Edward D. Stone showed what can be done when inventiveness is substituted for the traditionally heavy hand of official architecture. Its inner court (above) is an oasis of foliage and flashing water under the blazing Indian sun. John Carl Warnecke also uses water and native design elements in his graceful model for the projected embassy in Bangkok (opposite). Less dramatic than the buildings for hot countries but equally suited to its setting is Eero Saarinen's embassy designed for the cool northern light of London's Grosvenor Square (lower left).

LOUIS CHECKMAN; COURTESY *Life*

on a program unprecedented in the history of Federal construction. For the first time the nation's gifted corps of Modern architects has been entrusted with the designing of a whole series of embassies and consulates: buildings thoroughly contemporary in spirit which make full use of modern industrial technology.

In Washington itself, however, the latest major work of our Federal builders, the costly new Senate Office Building (shown on page 19) continues the dreary style of imitative classicism, complete with a mock portico that leads literally nowhere, since it provides no entrance to the building. By contrast the list of designers of the new embassies and consulates reads like an honor roll of contemporary American architects, including the pioneers Mies van der Rohe, Walter Gropius, and Richard Neutra, leaders of the new generation such as Eero Saarinen, Minoru Yamasaki, and Harry Weese, as well as gifted young men such as Vincent Kling and Paul Rudolph. Some of them are architects' architects —designers who receive comparatively little national publicity, such as John Lyon Reid of San Francisco, and Nicholas Satterlee and Chloethiel Smith of Washington,

D. C., but whose work belongs at a high international level.

What gives these new foreign buildings taken as a group, from Accra to Oslo, from Asunción to Teheran, their distinction is the civilized ease with which they take their places in ancient and sometimes exotic environments, at the same time conveying the dignity, strength, resourcefulness, and the idealism of the United States.

Architecture sheds light on national character in puzzling ways. At home, tapering with majestic strength as it rises 555 feet to the apex of its pointed cap, the Washington Monument stands solitary and immaculate as the focal point of the baroque Federal city. No structure—not even the maternal dome of the Capitol—is more identifiably "American," more grandly and simply "democratic," more profoundly representative of us, than this rigid and powerful shaft which commemorates the Father of His Country.

Or, at least, this is what the gigantic obelisk would seem to say, not only to Americans but to the world at large. Yet, as Joseph Hudnut, former dean of Harvard's School of Design, once pointed out in a fascinating study of the monument, other places under the sun have seen obelisks, includ-

Traditional Federal style is illustrated by the Vermont post office and courthouse above. Some of today's best, on home soil, is seen in an architect's rendering of "Number 9," a projected Washington office block (top); the new Air Force Academy (below); and models of a new Federal building in San Francisco (second from right) and New York headquarters for the U. S. Mission to the UN (far right).

ing those of old Egypt sacred to Ra, to which priests uttered incantations and before which solar rituals were performed that would cause acute discomfort to a modern American witnessing them. From Egypt the obelisk was literally transported to Rome, where it was installed on the long *spina* of the circus around which the chariots turned.

That an architectural form so ancient as the obelisk, with so authoritarian a history behind it, should inspire reverence in a democracy committed by its founders to adventure bravely into the future, is a matter to ponder. What, if anything beyond its mere location, makes the Washington Monument an American building? To be sure, it is the *biggest* obelisk ever erected; and admiration of size has long been an American characteristic.

The obelisk and the temple have one revealing characteristic in common. Both—although one was invented in Egypt and the other developed in Greece—were taken by Rome for her own, as were so many other imported art forms; and Rome, Henry Adams observed sourly, "is ourselves." The remark was tinged with irony, for it implied certain positive national virtues such as technological vigor and a hard streak of practicality, but it more clearly suggested the vices of plutocratic vulgarity, moral corruption, and imperial pretensions. The Rome of the Caesars seemed to be meant, but Adams did not exclude the Rome of the Renaissance popes. Did analogies exist with both? And what of the primitive, agrarian Rome which Cincinnatus left his plow to save?

Surely it bore some resemblance to the young Republic over which John Adams and Thomas Jefferson presided.

For, by paradox, it was Jefferson the democrat who did most to initiate America's official architectural romance with Rome. If today the Virginian is honored in Washington by a memorial which is at once a gross caricature of the Pantheon and a cruel copy of Monticello, some of the responsibility is his own.

The classicism of the early Republic—the "Greek Revival" —had no quarrel with technological progress: a masonry and carpentry tradition was still supreme, men built as they best could, and there was no inkling of the future complexity of industrial society. The change came in the course of the nineteenth century. Before the transition from republican to imperial Rome was effected, the nation had to increase in wealth and power, to impose its will over the breadth of the continent and the seas beyond, which it did with remarkable speed under the impetus of the Industrial Revolution.

Inexorably, Federal architecture underwent profound changes at the same time. A new taste for baroque splendor was displayed, notably in Thomas U. Walter's immense cast-iron dome of the Capitol. Then came the dense, heavy confusion of the "General Grant style," perfectly revealing the sad disorder of the administration in massive piles like the old State, War, and Navy Building. The full impact of the new imperial classicism did not strike the United States until the Chicago World's Fair of 1893. The American peo-

ple were astonished and delighted by the White City of plaster Renaissance palaces. To a nation still raw and unkempt, although it already possessed the masterful early skyscrapers of Louis Sullivan and the rest of the Chicago School, this glimpse of "higher culture" seemed the culmination of its pioneer strivings. Fully fifty years would pass, Sullivan predicted accurately, before the spell of the Beaux-Arts façade would begin to fade.

America was in for an age of "commercial classicism," the heyday of McKim, Mead, and White. Even in the "stage setting" of the fair, Louis Sullivan did not fail to note that "the structure representing the United States Government was of an incredible vulgarity." And after 1901, under the direction of the fair's moving spirit, Daniel H. Burnham, Washington itself was transformed into a White City that would be permanent.

During the thirties the capital's resemblance to Rome for the first time became discomforting to more Americans than a handful of Modern architects. Already in 1924 the young Lewis Mumford had warned that "architecture, like government, is about as good as a community deserves," and intimated that the nation led by Calvin Coolidge might be riding for a fall. When the depression struck, the pompous exteriors and the dreary, inefficient innards of the public buildings indicated to perceptive Americans that they deserved all they had got.

What seems most significant about the official architecture

of the thirties in retrospect was the universal decadence of style among the major powers. England remained lost in Georgian reverie. France devised a peculiarly weak "governmental modern," of which a leading example is the Palais de Chaillot. Only the Italian Fascists, who were enthusiastic practitioners of governmental modern (although they erected frankly classical monuments of almost incredible coarseness, too), for a time also gave lip service to serious Modern architecture, and thus kept some gifted men in the country. In Germany, on the other hand, which architecturally had been the most progressive large nation of the twenties, the Modern was rigorously prohibited by the Nazis. Thus America received, to its good fortune, such refugee masters as Gropius, Mies, and Eric Mendelsohn.

Their presence made the United States, already the home of Frank Lloyd Wright, the most powerful center of fine architecture in the world. The tide was changing, on a swell of public opinion, even though porticoes and colonnades continued to be erected by the government. Yet at the same time the government's own architects were accomplishing fine new work in the vast program of public improvements sponsored by the Roosevelt administration. Across the Tennessee Valley extended the magnificent spillway of Norris Dam, perhaps the finest and truest monument of the period: handsome in itself, splendidly placed in the landscape, and responsible for a transformation of the entire surrounding region through the power of its turbines. Norris proved what

Less pretentious Federal buildings, offering less scope for political interference, often have the best chance of achieving architectural distinction in America. An example is this airy umbrella over a Coast Guard swimming pool in Alameda, California, commissioned by local headquarters and designed by Ernest J. Kump.

some Modernists have doubted; namely, that a deliberately monumental treatment of a structure is altogether possible in the twentieth century, and that it can succeed without pretension or strain.

When the Second World War was over, the United States seemed ready to embark on the most sweeping architectural adventure in its history: the Modern stood prepared to remake the natural environment, if the nation would have it so.

Yet the Modern had to reckon with the accumulated dead weight of the official aesthetic. Another obstacle to any improvement in government architecture was a postwar policy of thrift which, after so much profligacy in the past, provided little more than basic shelter in new construction. At a time when private corporations, awakening to the Modern, were proceeding with generous projects such as Lever House, the government took the expedient of leasing buildings from profit-minded contractors. Interestingly enough, however, at this point world opinion—particularly intellectual opinion—had an effect on a nation whose attitude toward its own "eggheads" often verges on disdain.

As the United States assumed world-wide responsibilities of power, many foreign intellectuals not only questioned American political motives but undertook to scoff at American cultural pretensions. Yet our diplomatic installations abroad did little to make the American image winning. When they

ART HUPY

were not actually palatial accommodations of the Old Order, made over into embassies, as at Rome, they were banal imitations of the great monumental styles of the past, like most Federal architecture at home. But Europeans had the true Renaissance and baroque on every side for comparison; and a perceptive Parisian, for example, would see little in the embassy off the Place de la Concorde to indicate that his own time-softened civilization, admirably represented by the Hotel Crillon across the street, had much to learn from America in architecture, democracy, or anything else.

Nor were the embassies erected since the last war the kind of buildings which might inspire affection for the United States. Ostensibly they were Modern structures, but they often took their places brutally in hallowed Old World streets, notably in Brussels. Moreover, they were just not very good Modern, which like any style has many levels of quality. The heavy-handed new embassy at Rio de Janeiro—a place with plenty of fine contemporary architecture—was scarcely the sort of building to give the countrymen of Oscar Niemeyer an impression of American ability and friendliness.

In 1953 State Department officials and congressmen, so insensitive to their own accommodations in Washington, took indignant notice of the embassies at Brussels and Rio, and of similarly harsh structures going up at Havana and Madrid. The structures were denounced as miniature ver-

The National Park Service, long committed to the rustic log cabin, has now gone Modern—and the results have been distinguished. This is Anshen & Allen's new steel and concrete visitors' pavilion at Dinosaur National Monument in Utah. The glass shed provides a balcony view of the paleontological excavations.

sions of the UN Secretariat in New York and were deemed "cold" and excessively "international" in style. In short, the buildings were not "American."

But what *was* American? Critics of the UN Secretariat building have pointed out that its main failing, as public architecture, is that it too closely resembles an American commercial skyscraper designed to exploit land values with maximum rental return. Yet would it have been deeper in the native grain to return, as one diplomat suggested, to Colonial dormers and fanlights?

Clearly a new approach was needed, especially since Congress, as it can when piqued, appropriated no new foreign building funds. To the State Department's credit, an episode unique in the history of Federal architecture then occurred. Leading architects—not titular bigwigs, but some of the foremost designers in the country—were consulted, and their recommendations were actually heeded. In January, 1954, the department issued a declaration of policy for its Foreign Buildings Office which, if endorsed by the rest of the government, could well stand as a declaration of independence for our national architecture.

Henceforth, the directive specified, "distinguished" buildings were to be erected abroad which would "reflect credit on the United States," creating "goodwill by intelligent appreciation, recognition, and use of the architecture appropriate to the site and country." There would be no "adherence to any given style of architecture," a proviso which sounded the knell for neo-classicism, whose premise is that formal colonnades and pediments will make a building appropriate anywhere from the tropics to the arctic.

On the contrary, the way was open for the full diversity of the Modern, a movement which is never more winning than when the richness and depth of its *regional* possibilities come rationally into play. To make sure that genuinely appropriate and genuinely Modern buildings would be erected, the State Department set up a new kind of advisory panel within the FBO and accorded it unprecedented powers. The panel was to consist of one active, high-ranking career diplomat and three outstanding architects, who would serve at nominal pay for two years, when the membership would rotate in order to insure a continually fresh point of view.

That the department had serious intentions was clear from the stature of the architects named to the first panel: the superbly gifted Pietro Belluschi, and the older, less audacious, but extremely open-minded Ralph T. Walker and

CONTINUED ON PAGE 119

The American exhibit at the World Agricultural Fair in New Delhi this winter looks at first glance like a most stylish county fair, but Minoru Yamasaki's golden domes and reflecting pools owe more to India than to Indiana. This view of the model is from the rear, showing the garden exit and outdoor café. The main entrance is marked by flags at top center.

27

By JAMES RAMSEY ULLMAN

THE DREAM OF THE SOUTH SEAS

Pursued by generations

of Western men, its

idylls of escape

have produced both

high art and

disenchantment

A native's outrigger and fish traps at Punaauia,
Tahiti, tell of an Oceania still true to its myth.

Some dreams are private, our very own. Others are in the public domain. Over the past few centuries in our Western world, none, I think, has beguiled the minds of men more widely and persistently than the Dream of the South Seas.

It has beguiled mine, that I know; if not for centuries, for long enough. And it is therefore with a sense of fulfillment, of hopes long cherished and plans deferred, that I find myself, here and now, cruising at last through the fabled isles. Around me, as I stand at my ship's rail, are the blue waters, the green archipelagoes, the soft and shining wonder of the southern ocean. Below in my cabin, ready when needed (such as now) are paper, pencils, typewriter—the tools of my trade.

But there, in those tools and that trade, is the only rub, the only shadow. For I am well aware of how many fellow trades-men have preceded me on my path; how many novels and stories and poems and articles—plus songs and paintings and photographs and movies—have already been spawned by this world now around me. The South Seas Dream is no longer a young dream, least of all to writers and such. And the Johnny-come-lately cannot but wonder glumly if, in the whole of it, there can be a single fresh thought or image or word still left for the plucking.

Take words alone. "Lagoon" is a lovely one. So is "atoll." Who of us in his time has not conjured vicarious magic out of palm, breadfruit, pandanus, copra, schooner, outrigger, reef, trade wind, Kanaka, beachcomber, *pareu*, hula? But that is the trouble: we have conjured them too often. They have been written, composed, painted, and photographed into a huge, encompassing cliché—to the point where one hesitates to use the very phrase *South Sea Island* without a cough of apology.

As I step from my ship onto my long-dreamed Pacific out-post, a battalion of ghosts walk beside me. Their names (to list only the few who first catch the eye) are Melville and Ste-venson and Loti and London and Brooke and Maugham and

Meanwhile civilization has left such marks on the islands as these junked war planes on New Guinea.

Hall and Michener, and they eye me quizzically as if to ask, "Little man, what now?" From the shade of a coconut grove Gauguin peers over his easel with a sardonic smile. Down the beach, in the light of the moon (which rhymes with lagoon), the little brown girl in the little grass skirt glides from the little grass shack and wriggles her bottom.

I have come to the world of which Stevenson said it "touched a virginity of sense." But Stevenson did not have himself to contend with. Or scores of later best sellers. Or Hollywood, or Tin Pan Alley. Far from virginal, the South Seas now seems more of an old trollop, face bedaubed with stale words and images. And about the best the Johnny-come-lately can do is to look both trollop and ghost squarely in the eye and swear that he will not use either "languorous" or "paradise" more than once to a paragraph.

So now (new paragraph) I am on my languorous island. I am in paradise, or at least a fair facsimile thereof. And sitting beneath a cliché, beside a cliché, I ask myself why I am here; why all those here before me were here; just what it is that, over the years, has made this South Seas Dream so durable and potent.

In the beginning—for this Genesis—there was *not* the Word. There was the Fact. The Deed. The prehistoric migrations of the Pacific people—Melanesian, Micronesian, Polynesian—stand beyond comparison as the greatest of South Seas adventures; and if these ancient mariners had had a written language to record their voyages, we would today have an epic of more heroic proportions than the *Odyssey* or the Norse Eddas. There is no such record, however. There are only the shreds of chants and legends passed on by taletellers from generation to generation. As, for instance, *Seek ye the way. Though the distance be great, though the way be long, keep thy course, O son; across the waters is thy path.* . . . And beyond this there is only imagining, and the slow labors of anthropologists.

Presumably they were driven by the forces that have caused all the world's great migrations: fear of famine or plague or enslavement; hunger for land or food or freedom. They were not searching for paradise. They were searching for homes. And homes are what they found—homes in the myriad islands, which their descendants have now inhabited for so long that they have no record of any before them. But they, no less than Westerners, are human and have their dreams: their dream of paradise, which some call *Avaiki*. And it is not, to be sure, a South Sea Island, but the lost, forgotten land from which their ancestors once fled.

History, however, brought no great reverse migration. The Pacific's first discoverers remained to become, in turn, the discovered; and from the day, now four and a half centuries ago, when Magellan's ships pushed out into the southern ocean, their world was never to be the same again. By a freak of luck and navigation, Magellan himself, threading a course among thousands of islands, touched—indeed sighted—only Guam and a few of the adjoining Marianas. But after him came more ships and more men—Spanish, Portuguese, British, French, Dutch—beating inexorably out toward earth's farthest horizons. And along with Africa, Asia, and the Americas, the Pacific moved into the ken and dominion of Europe.

It was to be many years, however, before South Seas Discovery became South Seas Dream. For the early navigators and their patron kings back home, the dream was of Asia, of trade, wealth, and power of continental dimensions, and the islands were mere landmarks and staging posts on their journeys. Later came the true explorers, seeking the islands for their own sake: first Schouten and Le Maire and Tasman; then Wallis, Bougainville, La Pérouse, and, greatest of all, Captain James Cook. But they too were primarily on practical missions in the cause of science or empire-building or national prestige. And when in due time came the whalers and traders, blackbirders and missionaries, the motives at work were, if anything, even more remote from those of the searcher for Eden. Of them all, ironically, it was the missionary—in theory at least, a spiritual man—who was farthest afield from the true South Seas dreamer. For, far from seeking paradise in the distant islands, he was, on the contrary, convinced that he was bringing it with him.

Yet the dream, the legend, was germinating: through the records of exploration, through the tales of returned voyagers. And simultaneously, during the late eighteenth and early nineteenth centuries, the intellectual temper of Europe was changing in such a way as to make it ever more receptive. This was the age of the American and French Revolutions, of vast political and social upheaval; in literature, art, and music, of the ascendancy of romanticism over the older self-contained and rulebound classicism. For the first time since the High Renaissance, Western man was looking beyond the boundary of his own best-of-all-possible worlds, not in indifferent condescension but with wonder and desire, and in the world of the tropic islands found a new and almost irresistible magic.

There was a corollary influence at work as well; an influence that has surely grown no weaker with the passing of years. This was the revulsion of modern man against the complexity and fractiousness of the civilization he himself had created, and a consequent yearning for a simpler life. Here Rousseau was the intellectual bellwether, with his concept of "natural man" and "the noble savage"; and although he was never within thousands of miles of the Pacific, he was perhaps the prime artificer of the romantic mood which made the South Seas Dream possible.

Another early and influential apostle—also French—was Denis Diderot, who, stirred by the account of the travels of Bougainville, wrote a *Supplément* thereto; in it he presented Tahiti as an Eden beyond compare, beside whose dusky supermen—and -women—a European was a benighted clod. Diderot was chief of the Encyclopedists; therefore almost by definition a champion of fact. But here he was not interested in fact. He was interested in his thesis of the deca-

*In his retreat on Samoa in the 1890's Robert Louis Stevenson gave an American friend
this annotated photograph of himself, his family and retainers, including one cannibal.*

dence of Western civilization and the superiority of the "natural life"; and in its pursuit he created a Tahiti and Tahitians of almost total unreality. This, however, bothered neither him nor his host of readers. For his book was poetic, witty, titillating, and it made its point. In its wake, the South Seas Dream veered sharply off toward sheer fantasy; but, veering, it gained such strength and appeal that it was never to die.

Presently it was no longer Frenchmen only who were singing the South Seas Song. In England Lord Byron, prince of romantics, raised his voice in his rhapsodic "The Island"; and what Byron wrote Europe read—and cherished. Elsewhere other voices were heard: all lyric, all impassioned, and far more stimulating than the sober, often badly written accounts by the scribes and chroniclers of actual voyages. Looking out from the cold and fogbound north, from a world of war and want and confusion without end, the eye of man fixed upon an image it sorely needed—an image of peace, of beauty, of

Eden reborn. And thenceforth the South Seas Island was secure as dream and symbol.

Rousseau, Diderot, Byron, *et al*, were, to be sure, men who had "never been there." Indeed, for more than three centuries after Magellan, the Pacific remained unvisited by anyone who was primarily a writer, the firsthand accounts being those of sea captains and the assorted lieutenants and doctors, geographers and naturalists who accompanied them. Among the latter, during the 1830's, was no less an earth shaker than Charles Darwin, then a young scientist circling the world in the *Beagle*. But though Darwin was not insensitive to the spell of the Pacific ("Tahiti," he wrote, "must ever remain classical to the voyager in the South Seas"), he was primarily involved in a far different dream. And so too was Thomas Huxley, who, a decade later, followed a similar path.

As it developed, in the category of writers per se, the first in the field was not a European at all, but an American, Her-

TEXT CONTINUED ON PAGE 124

OVERLEAF: A PORTFOLIO IN COLOR GRAVURE OF PAUL GAUGUIN'S
SOUTH SEAS PAINTINGS, INTRODUCED BY MARSHALL B. DAVIDSON

THE ENIGMATIC ISLANDS OF PAUL GAUGUIN

By MARSHALL B. DAVIDSON

Shortly before his pitiful death in 1903, Paul Gauguin thought of quitting life in the South Seas to return to his native France. A hideous combination of afflictions—crippling eczema, syphilis, serious eye trouble, and alcoholism—was making a nightmare of the dream that had led him to his last lonely exile in the Marquesas. But for him there was to be no return.

Gauguin liked to think of himself as part savage, by nature inevitably at home among the primitive Polynesians who people so many of his paintings. For years he lived their life, in large measure, and he projected it in painted images that for most of us have fixed forever our vision of the wonder, the beauty, and the seduction of the South Seas. Inescapably, we tend to see that world as Gauguin chose to see it. He lamented the decadence and the corruption that had come to the islands with the white man; and he ignored them in his paintings—except, perhaps, as a reference in the undefinable melancholy that lingers throughout these tropic scenes. For the rest, he left us an idyll in which a mysterious tranquillity and a disquieting sensuousness are alike evoked in a radiance of exotic color.

To the end of his life Gauguin found his tawny island neighbors endearingly enigmatic. In his search for understanding he read a well-informed study of the islands and their people that had been written sixty years earlier, when the ancient myths and traditional observances of Oceania were still understood and revered by the natives themselves. His reading of that vanished past provided many of the allusions to strange gods, esoteric rituals, and primitive superstitions that appear in his paintings. He used them candidly as an artistic device, to set a

mood and complete a pattern that had little to do with ethnology and a great deal to do with the future of painting.

In a book of his own, Gauguin transcribed phrase after phrase from the earlier publication, crediting their wisdom and their eloquence to Tehura, his ingenuous early teenage mistress whose naked portrait appears in *The Spirit of the Dead Watches*. (All paintings referred to here are reproduced in the portfolio that follows.) Yet he painted the voluptuous little girl, he claimed, primarily as a study of the nude, placing her against a purple "background of terror" and dubbing in a very ordinary old woman as the watchful "ghost" to suggest the mysteriousness that continued to intrigue him in these people.

"My artistic center is in my head," Gauguin wrote his lawful wife shortly after he had moved to Tahiti—almost paradoxically for a man who had just journeyed halfway around the world to find new subjects. "I am not a painter who works from nature," he later elaborated. "With me everything happens in my wild imagination." As if to prove the point, he painted *The Day of the God*, one of his most effective Tahitian compositions, in Paris during his one trip home from the islands. The principal figure in the painting is Taaroa, creator of the world and central power in the Maori pantheon, about whom the artist had read and whom he here worked into a dreamlike effigy to anchor his design and to lend it enchantment.

In the islands, on the other hand, Gauguin borrowed from his own earlier work, from the paintings of his favorite European contemporaries, from the great Japanese print makers, and from whatever source would serve his "wild imagination" with convenient

motifs. The leering, claw-footed creature in the background of *Contes Barbares* revives a likeness of Meyer de Haan, a dwarfed Dutch companion of Gauguin's days in Brittany years before. His avowed deep admiration of Japanese prints is reflected in the flat patterns and raised perspective of *The White Horse*, as it is throughout his work.

Gauguin brought with him from Europe a collection of photographs that included reproductions of Javanese, Indian, and classical bas-reliefs, which he described as "a small world of companions who shall speak to me every day"—as indeed they did. The two native women who adore Mary and Jesus in *Ia Orana Maria* are "lifted" from figures in the sculptured frieze of a Javanese temple, a photograph of which Gauguin had treasured from the Paris World's Fair of 1889. Elsewhere sculptured horsemen from the Parthenon, white-clad girls from Egyptian painted reliefs, and other reminders of distantly remote originals find their way into his island pictures.

But whatever he borrowed, Gauguin translated into a unique language of his own invention, a language of flat, brilliant colors that he juxtaposed in decorative patterns without regard for precedent or probability. With fierce independence he insisted on his right to "dare everything," and in doing so to win the same right for all who followed him. What he abstracted from nature by "dreaming before it," as he said he did, had no literal meaning. The importance of his paintings was precisely in what was *not* expressed, in the pure poetry and "music" of his designs. In his South Seas paintings his daring reached a climax and firmly established his influence over the direction of modern art.

PHOTOGRAPHS OF NUMBERS 2, 3, AND 4 BY FRANK LERNER

CONTES BARBARES

MATAMOE

MAHANA no Atua

IA ORANA MARIA

Thucydides' War

Other ancient conflicts are lost in mists of legend, but the Peloponnesian War has been kept alive for twenty-four centuries by one man's passionate search for truth

By M. I. FINLEY

Normally the fame of ancient wars is fashioned by myth and romance. Helen of Troy, the Pass of Thermopylae, Alexander, Hannibal—these are the people and the incidents that keep wars alive. But not so the Peloponnesian War, fought between Athens and Sparta from 431 to 404 B.C. (with a seven-year break in the middle). It lives on not so much for anything that happened or because of any of the participants, except for Alcibiades in a minor key, but because of the man who wrote its history, Thucydides the Athenian. No other historian can match this achievement; no other war, or for that matter no other historical subject, is so much the product of its reporter.

That is achievement enough. It becomes even greater when we look more closely at the man and his book. All that we know about Thucydides is found in the few scraps he tells us himself and in an eccentric biography credited to Marcellinus. But clearly he was a humorless, not very lovable man—pessimistic, skeptical, highly intelligent, superficially cold and reserved, but with strong inner tensions which occasionally broke through the impersonal tone of his writing in savage whiplash comments. He wrote in a complicated, crabbed style, neither pleasant nor easy to read. Of few if any other of the world's greatest writers can it be said that they read better in translation than in the original. He refused to make the slightest concession to his audience, whether in style or in treatment of the subject. Nothing mattered but the events and the issues; these he would get right by persistent devotion to accuracy and understanding, and he would report his findings plain. Let the reader who wants romance go elsewhere, he says, I am not writing for the applause of the moment, but for all time.

He was a young man, probably in his late twenties, when the war began. Immediately, he perceived that this would be war on an unprecedented scale, and he decided to become its historian. How he went about his self-assigned task we do not know, for he says very little about his methods apart from a famous brief passage on the unreliability of eyewitness testimony. My narrative, he writes, "rests both on what I saw myself and on the reports of others, after careful research aiming at the greatest possible accuracy in each case. My conclusions have been reached with effort because eyewitnesses disagree about the same occurrence, from imperfect memory or from bias." He never names his informants, and on only two occasions does he say that he was a direct participant. It is left to us to conjure up a picture of Thucydides seeking out a vast number of witnesses from both sides, cross-questioning them closely, deciding on their veracity, piling up notes, sorting out the data, selecting and thinking and writing. He read whatever there was to be read, but that would have been very little, for this was a world of talk, not of writing. Basically, everything—the debates in the assembly, the embassies, the behind-the-scenes maneuvers, the battles—had to be reconstructed from what he was told or had witnessed.

As an able-bodied Athenian citizen, Thucydides was of course not free to give all his time to his project. This was a war in which everyone was mobilized. But in 424 he was exiled on a charge of failure to carry out properly an assignment as commander in the northeast. It is characteristic of him that he reports this fact briefly and without comment, except to add that he was in a better position thereafter to obtain information from both sides. His paternal ancestors had connections in Thrace and he retained property there, which enabled him to go on with his work at leisure. He lived through the entire war, was apparently permitted to return to Athens when it ended, and died not many years later.

When he died, someone (his daughter, one tradition has it) published the manuscript exactly as he left it, and there are some very puzzling aspects about the shape of the work at that stage. The whole of the last book is utterly unlike the preceding seven: it has the look of a collection of notes, organized but not worked up. It breaks off abruptly in the year 411 B.C., nearly seven years before the war ended. One might reasonably surmise that Thucydides had stopped writing when he reached that point in his story. However, there are substantial portions early in the volume that could not have been written until after 404, such as the discussion of the exact dating of the war and its duration. Thucydides was obviously working away at his *History* long after 411. But instead of continuing with the narrative, he revised and refashioned some of the earlier parts, and he wrote long chunks in them for the first time. There can be little doubt, for example, that both the Funeral Oration, which Pericles is said to have delivered in the first year of the war, and his last speech, in 430, were written by Thucydides not contemporaneously but nearly thirty years later. They are the old historian's retrospective views of the strength and great possibilities of Athens when the war began, written in the light of his city's complete, and unnecessary, defeat. And even earlier, in the first book with its detailed account of the incidents leading up to the war, there are some sentences that look very much like marginal notes Thucydides had made for himself, for still further recasting and rewriting.

We shall never know what was going on in Thucydides' mind in those final years; what it was that drove him back to the earlier years at the cost of a complete neglect of the ending. It is necessary to make some sort of reasonable guess, however, in order to get at his thinking in general. There is not a sentence in the book that states explicitly what Thucydides thought history was about, why it was important to write an accurate history of the war, or why that history would be a "possession for all time." These were far from obvious questions in his day, for the simple reason that the writing of history had scarcely begun. The Greeks were deeply attached to their past, but it was the distant past, the age of heroes, which attracted them and which they never tired of learning about from Homer and the tragic poets. For the rest, popular traditions served well enough—the stories about Solon and the tyrants and a handful of other figures. No doubt these stories were not very accurate, but what did that matter? Myths and half-truths performed the two necessary functions: they gave the Greeks a feeling of continuity, of nationhood, and they were the source of religious and moral teaching. Neither of these purposes required precise chronology, accurate detail, or complete documentation. In short, there seemed to be no need for history as the modern world understands it, or as Thucydides understood it.

To be sure, there were skeptics and rationalists who were dissatisfied. They neither believed in the philandering of Zeus and the crookedness of Hermes nor approved of a moral code with so unreliable a foundation. By Thucydides' time a considerable line of philosophers had been challenging the whole mythical structure and developing newer and more advanced systems of metaphysics and ethics on rational bases. However, it was not from such concerns that the impulse came for the writing of history, but from the political situation of fifth-century Greece. Herodotus was born and brought up in Halicarnassus, across the Aegean Sea from Athens, in that part of the Greek world which was in closest contact with the "barbarians," and which for many years had been subject to the Persians and before them to the Lydians. There a body of writing had grown up consisting of descriptions of manners and customs, geography, and fragments of history. Herodotus apparently planned another such work and traveled very widely collecting the necessary information. But then he came to Athens, was completely enthralled by it, and was inspired to an altogether new vision of his vocation. A generation earlier the Persians had mounted two great invasions of the Greek mainland, and had been driven back, heavily defeated against all the odds, thanks largely to the moral and practical leadership given by the Athenians. This was a heroic tale as worthy as that of the Trojan War, and it would soon be lost from memory unless it were fixed in writing. And so Herodotus wrote the first book about Greek history.

Thucydides read it and was tremendously impressed. He saw, as virtually no other contemporary saw, that Herodotus had made a very great discovery—namely, that it was possible to analyze the political and moral issues of the time by a close study of events, of the concrete day-to-day experiences of society, thereby avoiding the abstraction of the philosophers on the one hand and the myths of the poets on the other. He saw, too, that the struggle between Athens and Sparta had something of the epic quality of the Persian Wars and was equally profound in its meaning and its consequences. It was worth the whole of a man's life, he thought, to master the unfolding events in all their detail, their complexity, and their deepest meanings.

Thucydides began with an enormous advantage over Herodotus. The latter had had to re-create, for the most part, the atmosphere and the events of a period long past (though some of the battles between the Greeks and the Persians took place when he was a boy), whereas Thucydides was a contemporary and an actual participant. He then set himself a standard of accuracy which, commonplace as it may seem today, was quite extraordinary in the fifth century B.C. "So few pains," he complained, "do most men take in the inquiry for the truth, preferring to accept the first story that comes to hand." Only one possible model comes to mind, the Hippocratic school of medicine which was then at its height on the island of Cos. But even this will not explain why Thucydides transferred this passion for accuracy to the field of history. Like all such personal matters, the question defies explanation. Whatever the reason, it left him an exceedingly lonely figure in the history of ancient historical writing, for not one man after him, among either the Greek historians or the Roman, shared his passion. In this sense, Thucydides' kind of history was a dead-end street. Only among a few scientists, Aristotle and his disciples, for example, do we find anything comparable, and they never took history seriously.

From the beginning, too, Thucydides took still another extraordinary step. Human history, he decided, was a strictly human affair, capable of analysis and understanding entirely in terms of known patterns of human behavior, without the intervention of the supernatural. It is impossible to say what his religious beliefs were, except that he detested the soothsayers and oracle-mongers who were a plague in wartime Athens. As a historian he recognized their existence in several brief, utterly contemptuous remarks. Otherwise, apart from a few not easily explained references to Fortune (*Tyche*), his *History* unfolds without gods or oracles or omens. On this score it is scarcely credible that the lives of Herodotus and Thucydides overlapped—yet we know they did.

These were matters of fundamental outlook, and they gave Thucydides' work its tone. But they could not provide the techniques. How does one go about writing the history of a long war? Thucydides had no precedent to fall back on, no book, no teacher from whom he could learn the business of being a historian. Not even Herodotus, for he was too diffuse, interested in too many things, while Thucydides proposed to concentrate very narrowly on the war and its politics. Apart from everything else, this difference in scale and intensity made Herodotus an unsatisfactory model.

For instance, consider something as elementary as dates. We say that the Peloponnesian War began in 431 B.C. An Athenian had to say that it began in the archonship of Pythodorus, which was meaningless to a non-Athenian, and indeed even to Athenians twenty or thirty years later, unless they had a list of the archons (who held office for only one year) before them while they read. In a large-scale war, furthermore, with many things happening in different places at the same time, dating by years alone would not give the right kind of picture for Thucydides. All the little connections and sequences, the day-to-day causes and consequences would be lost. Introducing months would not help. Every city had its own calendar: the names of the months were not all alike, nor was the order, nor even the time of the new year. To write a coherent narrative, therefore, Thucydides had to invent a system. After fixing the beginning of the war, he dated all subsequent events first by counting the number of years that elapsed from the start, and then by dividing each war year into halves, which he labeled summer and winter. Simple enough, yet the scheme was unique and the difficulties in making it work are nearly unimaginable today.

Fixing the beginning was almost the hardest problem of all. Wars do not erupt out of nothing on one particular day. The first shot or the formal declaration of war can conveniently be called the beginning of a war, but cannot be the beginning of its history. How far back must the historian go? That is a most critical decision for him; on it depends the interpretation he presents to his readers. In the two decades between 1919 and 1939, three radically different views of the causes of World War I prevailed, in turn, among students of modern history. Each required its own account of the prehistory of the war. Likewise, in late fifth-century Athens there were sharp disagreements about the causes of the Peloponnesian War, and there were, no doubt, similarly conflicting views elsewhere in the Greek world.

Thucydides sorted out the essential from the casual, the primary causes from the more immediate grievances and the pretexts. The latter he wrote up in very great detail, devoting the whole of the first book to the background. The result is clear, brilliant, and yet somehow unsatisfactory. Thucydides himself was never satisfied with it. Ideas which seemed right early in the war lost their persuasiveness twenty or twenty-five years later. From that distance in time the grievances of Corinth over Corcyra and Potidaea, for example, no longer loomed so large. The Athenian empire had a different look, even retrospectively, after it was broken apart; so did Pericles, after a succession of leaders like Cleon and Hyperbolus, for whom Thucydides felt a contempt and an anger that he does not disguise. More and more it was pure politics, power against power, the rights and wrongs, the morality of power, which seemed the only important and permanent elements in the picture, with the concrete details mere exemplifications. "The truest cause," he came to believe, was this: "The growth of the power of Athens and the alarm which it inspired in Sparta made war inevitable."

Sorting out, selecting what goes into and what is to be excluded from the mass of available data, highlighting and underscoring—these are of course what the historian, any historian, does all the time. Consciously or not, he is applying his personal canons of relevance, and that means his ideas about the nature of politics, of social behavior, in a word, about history. Even when a historian is explicit and tells us what he thinks history is about, he is judged not so much by his theoretical remarks as by the work itself. Thucydides tells us nothing, so that only the work in the form in which he left it reveals his thinking. And the work is, in a sense, self-contradictory; the historian seems to be pulling, and to be pulled, in opposite directions all the time.

On the one hand, there is a passion for the most minute detail: minor commanders, battle alignments, bits of geography, and the like, so that a mere index of names occupies thirty-two double column small octavo pages. On the other hand, there are astonishing gaps and silences, whole chunks of history that are left out altogether or dismissed in a phrase or odd sentence. For example, there is a marvelous account of the brutal civil war between the oligarchic and democratic factions in Corcyra in 427 B.C., but scarcely a mention of other such struggles (until the oligarchic coup in Athens in the year 411). Yet it is obvious that internal faction played an important part all through the history of the war, and Thucydides himself knew it and stressed it. Then there is the famous contradiction between the narrative, to which he applies all his powers and discipline in the search for total accuracy, and the speeches, in which he brings out the central issues and conflicts *as he saw them*—but not necessarily as the speakers saw them, and surely not exactly as the speakers expressed them. In such a case as the debate about Mytilene in the third book, it is easy to demonstrate that Thucydides knowingly distorted that day's meeting in the Athenian assembly.

He was a genius, and he was a dedicated man. Easy explanations therefore will not do. His difficulties lay very deep; to this day they remain the essential difficulty of all historical writing, and it is the mark of Thucydides' greatness that he appreciated it so early, at the very beginning of historiography. The historian's data are individual events and persons whose sum total is the historical process. Unlike the poet, he must get them right, exactly as they were, and not, in Aristotle's phrase about tragedy, as they might or ought to have been "from probability or necessity." But then what? A mere retelling of individual events in sequence, no matter how accurately captured, would be just that and nothing more. Greek intellectuals like Thucydides believed that knowledge for its own sake was meaningless, its mere accumulation a waste of time: knowledge must lead to understanding. In the field of history that meant trying to grasp general ideas about human behavior, in war and politics, in revolution and government. Thucydides' problem, in short, was to move from the particular to the universal, from the concrete events to the underlying patterns and generalities.

Undoubtedly, Thucydides did not grasp the complexity of the problem right at the start, nor did he ever find a solution that fully satisfied him. He was constantly probing and experimenting, trying out techniques and refining them. To insure maximum accuracy, he kept his narrative sections rather impersonal, making infrequent comments and allowing the story to unfold by itself. Then, to lay bare what stood behind the narrative, the moral and political issues, the debates and disagreements over policy, the possibilities and the mistakes and the motives, his main device was the speech. Sometimes he chose a single speech out of a number which were made in an assembly or conference, sometimes a pair, which by their diametrical opposition presented the sharpest possible choice of actions. These speeches are in direct discourse, and are very much abridged—a perfectly legitimate procedure. But they are also, without exception, written in the language and style of Thucydides, and that gives the modern reader, at least, some twinges of conscience.

In fact, the speeches in Thucydides raised grave doubts among ancient critics as well. Their effectiveness is beyond doubt: the total impact is overwhelming. The reader is quite carried away; not only does he feel that he has seen the Peloponnesian War from the inside, but he is certain that he knows exactly what the issues were, why things happened as they did. More than that, his understanding seems to come from the actors themselves, not from the historian. To Thucydides' contemporaries, far more than to us, this seemed a natural and intelligible procedure. No people have elevated talk and debate into a way of life as did the ancient Greeks. They talked all the time, in public and in private, and they talked with enthusiasm and persuasiveness. Their literature was filled with talk, from the long speeches and monologues of the *Iliad* and the *Odyssey* to the equally long speeches and debates in Herodotus. And in the very years of the Peloponnesian War there was Socrates, who did nothing *but* talk—a philosopher without parallel, for he never wrote a line in all his long life. But no enlightened reader of Homer or Herodotus believed for one moment that the speeches recorded in their books were anything but the creations of the author, whereas Thucydides gave the impression that he was reporting, not creating.

Even Thucydides' warmest admirers must concede that the speeches, which make up a substantial portion of the work as a whole, are not reporting in the same sense as the narrative. The process of selection has gone too far: the historian has taken responsibility not only for choosing the salient points from actual speeches but also for having the "speakers say what was in my opinion demanded of them by the various occasions." That is what Thucydides often did in the speeches. No one can be certain of his motives in so doing, of course; but given his great integrity and dedication, it seems to me that the only satisfactory explanation for this odd procedure was his desire to penetrate to the final and general truths, his fear that they would not emerge from the details unless he underscored and heightened them in this way. How successful he was is shown by the fact that, to this day, the image of Pericles or Cleon that the world preserves is the one Thucydides created by means of the speeches he had them make.

In a sense Thucydides was too successful. He left no ground for re-examination or alternative judgment. So ruthless was he in stripping away whatever he thought was "romance," or irrelevance, that we are disinclined to evaluate Cleon, for example, in any way but Thucydides' own. This man led Athens for several years after the death of Pericles, but Thucydides gives him four appearances only, one of them restricted to a single sentence and one a speech. The picture that emerges is complete and dramatic—but is it right? We do not know. More than that, the picture is intended to represent not only Cleon but the demagogue as a type, the kind of leader who took over when Pericles died and, in the historian's judgment, led Athens to folly and de-

struction. Having summed up Cleon, Thucydides ignored the others, just as he summed up civil strife in general by one example, that of Corcyra.

No historian has ever surpassed Thucydides in this ability to portray a typical figure or situation, and to do so without seeming to intervene in any significant measure. Pericles' Funeral Oration, the plague, the party conflict in Corcyra, the debate between Cleon and Diodotus over what to do with rebellious Mytilene, the account of the oligarchic coup of 411 B.C.—these are what make the book a "possession for all time." The continuous narrative in which they are embedded has another quality and another interest. Without it the big scenes and the main ideas would lose their persuasiveness. It is the painstaking accuracy of the narrative that makes the rest seem so real and convincing. On the other hand, Thucydides was right in his feeling that the mere piling up of details, no matter how carefully chosen and described, would eventually lose its interest. The combination he discovered survives because it is particular and universal at the same time, and because it is in the last analysis a moralist's work.

Thucydides was not an original thinker. The general ideas with which he was obsessed were few and simple. He took a pessimistic view of human nature and therefore of politics. Some individuals and some communities, by their moral qualities, are entitled to positions of leadership and power. But power is dangerous and corrupting, and in the wrong hands it quickly leads to immoral behavior, and then to civil strife, unjust war, and destruction. These are the age-old themes of poets and philosophers. The genius of Thucydides lay in his effort to present them in this new way, by writing contemporary history. In some respects he alone of the ancient historians has a modern (or better, a nineteenth-century) quality: in his concentration on war and politics to the virtual exclusion of everything else, in his research methods, in his concern for the most minute detail. Yet he permitted himself liberties, as I have indicated, which no respectable modern historian would dream of. He did this because he apprehended the limits of history, of the study of specific, concrete events, as well as its possibilities, and he wanted desperately to transcend them. Whether he succeeded without becoming something other than a historian, whether it is possible to succeed in such an endeavor, remains an open question in the study of history.

M. I. Finley is a university lecturer in classics at Jesus College, Cambridge. He is the author of The World of Odysseus *and edited* The Greek Historians, *published last year.*

Zen Telegrams

DRAWINGS BY PAUL REPS

Paul Reps is a native American who has traveled much in the Orient and steeped himself in Zen Buddhist ways. For some time he contented himself with modestly giving his drawings to his friends, calling them "weightless gifts," or "poems before words." Then an exhibition of them was arranged in Kyoto, a gallery sign quoting these prices: "1,000 yen each to automobile owners . . . 100 yen to anyone poor . . . 10 yen to lovers of Buddha." The show was immediately successful and others quickly followed. Last year the Charles E. Tuttle Company of Rutland, Vermont, and Tokyo published a selection of them under the title *Zen Telegrams*. The title is apt, for Reps's intention is to speed his message to the heart with the succinctness of Morse Code and with the pricking insistence of a Zen *koan*, or baffling conundrum. With his brush he seeks to obtain the quality of Japanese calligraphic ideographs. Occasionally his picture-word images echo in the mind in the way that Zen dialogues do—like the shreds of improbable dreams remembered.

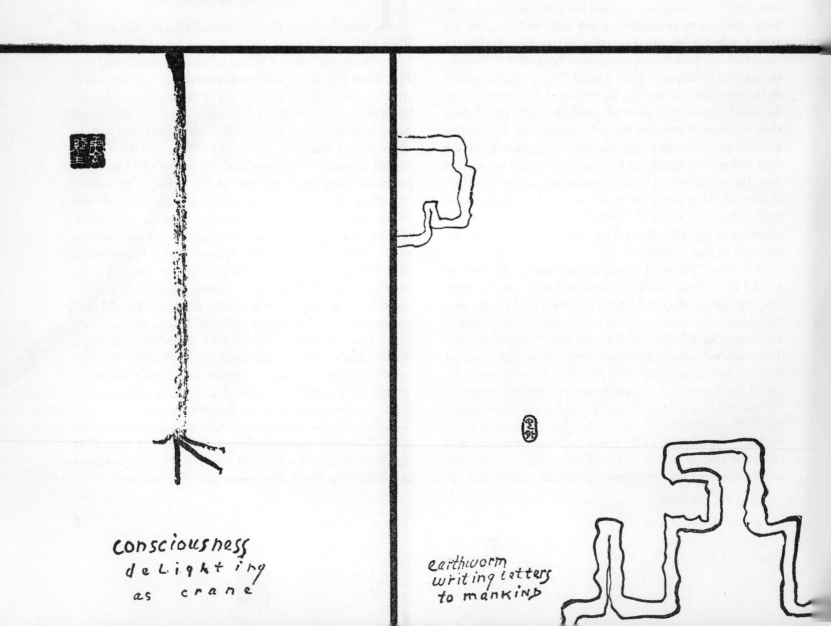

consciousness
deLighting
as crane

earthworm
writing letters
to mankind

rocks preaching
Become some
Silent sound

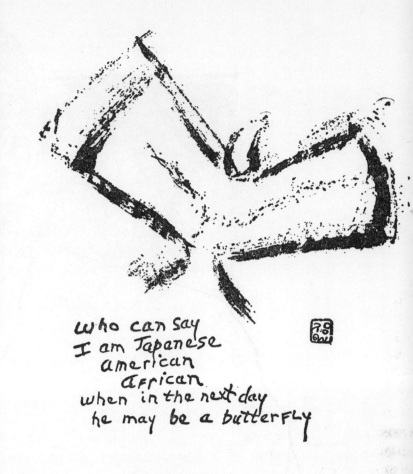

who can say
I am Japanese
american
african
when in the next day
he may be a butterfly

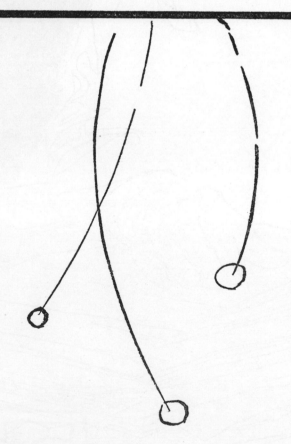

captured
snowflakes
suffering

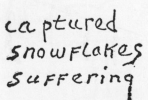

pine drinking
Luminous dew
as if nothing
had happened

THE ARTIST SPEAKS FOR HIMSELF
Another in a series of interviews with leading creative personalities conducted under the guest editorship of George Plimpton. Earlier subjects were Ernest Hemingway (January, 1959) and Larry Rivers (September, 1959)

Archibald MacLeish:
On Being a Poet in the Theater

Archibald MacLeish has published poems for more than forty years, has twice received the Pulitzer Prize for poetry, and has long been recognized as a major figure in contemporary letters—a position greatly enhanced by his triumphant *J.B.*

A play in verse is not box office. Neither is a play with a Biblical theme. A play which opens the night the newspapers go on strike (as New York's did on December 12, 1958), so that the critic's reviews cannot be circulated, doesn't have a chance. Yet *J.B.* proved stronger than its adversities, and had a ten-month Broadway run before going on an extended tour. When Brooks Atkinson of *The New York Times* wrote his review of the first night (for the newspaper that wasn't printed) he called *J.B.* "one of the memorable works of the century." Elia Kazan's direction, and the acting of Christopher Plummer, Raymond Massey, and Pat Hingle were widely praised. To no one's surprise, *J.B.* provided Archibald MacLeish with his third Pulitzer Prize—this time in the category of drama.

The scene of the play is a circus tent, where two vendors, Mr. Zuss and Nickles, impersonate God and Satan while J.B., an American businessman, suffers the afflictions of Job in a circus ring that represents the world. At the end of the play, J.B. accepts the return of his prosperity from God, but rejects blind obedience to Him in favor of reverence for life—a conclusion which has stirred much controversy.

Its author is a lean and athletic man, whose face is nearly unwrinkled, and whose gestures express a consistent energy. His speech is rapid, hearty, and generous. The interview took place at Uphill Farm, in Conway, Massachusetts, the summer home which MacLeish bought in 1927, on returning from six years abroad among the young postwar expatriates. The farm is a steep quarter mile up from the center of Conway, and it seems to overlook the trees and hayfields of all Massachusetts.

INTERVIEWER: You were saying before lunch that the production of *J.B.* was the greatest . . .

MACLEISH: . . . the greatest educational experience of my life. You don't usually start a new career at the age of sixty-six, which I was in the fall of '58. To move into, first of all, a new world, the world of the theater; secondly, to move into it as friend and companion of a great master of the art, as Kazan is, and in company with him to commit yourself to the task—you're not just sitting watching a demonstration, you're in it, by God! I don't know that I passed the examination, but believe me I was there!

INTERVIEWER: I want to ask you a few things about this experience in a little while, but before I do, maybe you can tell me how it came about. In the first place, why does a modern poet with a major reputation want to write for the stage? Yeats and Eliot, as well as you, have wanted to.

MACLEISH: I can't answer for anyone else. For myself it's a question of the hero. The hero of the lyric is Me, and Me seems to get smaller and more self-conscious and more strident as the world gets fuller and fuller of people and things and gas fumes and advertisements—all the noise and nonsense. Whereas the hero of a play—a play in poetry at least—is Him. And Him is more interesting—less preoccupied with himself anyway.

A little while before he died, Maxwell Anderson told me his years in the theater had persuaded him that a man could say on the stage or for the stage *anything* he had to say, private or public—public as well as private. And this seems to me to be completely true, and to be one of the reasons why poets aspire to the stage. One of the problems for anybody writing poetry at this time is to find a means that will let you say your hayload of saying—that will enable you to get on paper what you want to get on paper, to get into words what you want to get into words. A play will let you do that, or should if you have any kind of control of the medium. Drama is a means of enabling you to say your say to that imaginary audience which isn't yourself but which is somebody who has your questions and wants the answers.

INTERVIEWER: What is it in the form that allows you to say more than you can say in a poem?

MACLEISH: The other voice. You have

An interview by DONALD HALL

49

many, many voices, and you're moving always to different voices. These voices, although they are the voices of characters whom you have yourself conceived, are nevertheless the voices of characters who take on identities of their own, and who gradually people the play and take it over. Then you can have, as you could never have in a lyric poem, the real conflict of will, which is a conflict of purposes, not a conflict of interests.

That is one way your question can be answered. Another thing about the form is the relation of dramatic writing to time. I suppose a lyric poem exists at all times or any time or every time. It is inconceivable to me that there could be or should be a play which had its locus in "time-always." It has to have its locus *some*time. Its instant may be universal, but at the same time its universal is instant, and therefore more immediate and therefore more communicative.

INTERVIEWER: Then how does a verse play differ from a prose play? Do you have theories like T. S. Eliot? Theories of structure, perhaps?

MACLEISH: I have theories, but I don't think I could state them in terms of structure. Let me indulge in a few didactic remarks that I probably couldn't defend if I were put up against a wall. I can't conceive of a "realistic" play, in the modern sense of "realistic," being done in verse. I can't see any good reason for doing such a play in verse; in fact I think verse would get in the way. It seems to me that the justification for verse on the stage—if a justification is needed, and I think one usually is—is found when you are dealing with material which has an added dimension—a shadow, you might say.

Take a play based upon or relating to a mythical situation, where the *implications* are "always"—universal. The difference is this: history is something that is true at a given place and time. Myth is something that is true at any place and time: true then and therefore true forever; true forever and therefore true then. If you could go back in history, you could change history, because history has elements of choice. But if you went back into myth you couldn't change anything. If you enter the myth, you move with the story. This means that your dramatic time in such a play would be of a rather different order from chronological time. Your dramatic time *includes* "always." And "always" exists in poetry rather than prose. Poetry can introduce it into the play. And the play will reciprocate by giving the poetry space. Another way of saying it is that in prose you must be plau-

sible. You must persuade plausibly. In poetry, once you've established the poetic dimension, you don't need to be plausible. You have a greater freedom of flight. I think it's somewhere in there that you get the justification.

INTERVIEWER: How is it then that Shakespeare could write history plays in verse?

MACLEISH: A good question! Maybe because his subjects are all of them far enough away. The great ones are far enough away in historical time, far enough away in dimensions like grandeur of person and grandeur of event, so that they take on the aspect, at least, of the mythical. Perhaps one would have to find a different word than myth; perhaps one would have to talk in terms of the heroic or the generalizable. I just don't know.

INTERVIEWER: I wonder if your theory of subject matter isn't really a theory of language. Isn't this what you were getting at in *The New York Times* when you said, "I badly needed an ancient structure on which to build the contemporary play that has haunted me for five years past"? You needed this ancient structure in order to be able to use poetic language, didn't you?

MACLEISH: No. Yes. Now let me be sure that I say exactly what I mean to say. Not to be able to *use* poetry but to give poetry room to work on the stage. I needed the myth for the sake of that remove from the event which makes it possible to perceive the *kind* of significance, the largeness of significance, which poetry can bring to dramatic life. I wasn't looking for an excuse for writing verse.

INTERVIEWER: Does the process of writing a play differ, for you, from the process of writing a long poem? Do you use stage models? Do you have movement of characters in mind?

MACLEISH: I had a stage in mind from the very beginning, when I wrote *J.B.* Actually it's pretty much the stage that was later realized, first by Donald Oenslager at Yale, and then by Boris Aronson in New York. But if you mean, did I think about it in terms of entrances and exits, position on the stage, and so forth, I never did. Actually, after my experience with *J.B.*, I would be inclined to say that it's just as well not to give much thought to position on the stage. This is the sort of thing that a director has to control. The first thing that Kazan did was to forget my stage directions. He wanted the stage directions to be the expression of his modeling of the entire action on the stage, and not descriptive adjuncts to the printed text.

INTERVIEWER: What about the actual process of writing?

MACLEISH: I began writing the play about five years before it was produced. I took off, not as a playwright but as a writer, from a preoccupation that wouldn't let me alone. It was a preoccupation certainly not unique in my mind, the extraordinary disasters that had befallen mankind in the ten or fifteen years just past, a period during which I suppose more innocents found themselves maimed, hurt, mutilated, destroyed than ever before in the world's history. You couldn't think about it at all without thinking in terms of the incomprehensible injustice of the experience of our time, the experience of all times, of this universe itself. It was actually when I went down to West Ham in the East End of London after the Battle of Britain that these things began eating at me.

I took off from that and, as nearly as I can reconstruct it, I moved next to the great myth. I didn't start with the conception of doing anything about Job. I started with this preoccupation, and then it occurred to me that the myth of Job was the great myth of this experience. And I moved from that to the questions that are bothering me now in another connection: How do you bring a great world myth into focus? How do you relate it to *now*? You see the relation, but how do you get it clear *dramatically*?

Finally, after the play was largely written in other terms, I suddenly hit on the conception of taking two old actors working in the circus (they were both old then), and turning them into my protagonists, one of them trying to play God and the other trying to play Satan.

I think that's roughly the order in which it went. First the preoccupation with an experience, then a sense of the illustrative myth, then the problem of how to relate the myth to a contemporary situation, then the solution of that problem, and then the writing of the play.

INTERVIEWER: I'd like to ask you about the earlier production. How many performances did the play have at Yale and in Europe? It was the same production, wasn't it, that was taken to Brussels? Is the text like the printed text? How did Oenslager's set differ from Aronson's?

MACLEISH: It was played at Yale for a week. Directed by Curt Canfield with student actors. Beautifully done. It was this production that went to the World's Fair at Brussels, where it was produced first, as I understand it (I wasn't there), in a small theater as part of a sort of contest between amateur theatrical groups from all over, and then it was done for a number of performances—maybe as many as seven, I don't know—in the big American theater in Brussels. The performance in Brussels was the same as the one at Yale, and the text was the same as the printed text except for numerous cuts: the play as printed is too long. One principal difference between the sets was that Oenslager's was a brand-new circus tent, brand-new everything in it, and Aronson's is old, battered, beat up—had always existed and always would. If Aronson's was right and Oenslager's wrong, in this regard, it was my fault and not Oenslager's. Until I began thinking about the play in terms of the kind of production that eventually resulted in New York, I never realized how much the antiquity of that circus meant, how important it was that the tent should be old. Oenslager's set was handsome and it worked.

INTERVIEWER: Perhaps I could ask you first about the Broadway production by asking about the start of it. You opened during the newspaper strike of last December. Did you have trouble?

MacLeish: We had had a very tough time in Washington. We just about had the play swinging along when we got to New York—just as the newspaper strike was set to get started. The hope that the strike might be avoided grew thinner and thinner as time went by. The day before we opened I remember running into Kazan and our producer, Alfred de Liagre, Jr., in the lobby of the ANTA Theatre, both sitting there glumly, and saying, "Well, we've really had it. There'll be a strike tomorrow, and then nothing in the world can save us." We had spent about all the money we had. It really looked as though we'd close in three, four, five days. I didn't know enough to be scared. So I assured both these experienced gentlemen that this cloud had a silver lining, that if things were as bad as they seemed to be, they would have to be better before long.

Actually, it turned out that way. We opened and then the cast and everyone went to a nearby Chinese restaurant. The drama critics, like good fire horses, went on writing their reviews during the strike. They never knew when their newspapers were going to open, but whether they opened or not, their reviews were going to be on record. Along about two o'clock in the morning, these reviews began coming in, and we discovered that the critics liked the play. All of them. And there we were, "In" as they say on Broadway. And nobody knew it but us, and we were in a Chinese restaurant.

I had been asked three or four weeks before to go on Dave Garroway's television show the next morning, and I'd accepted, under the urgings of our pressman, without stopping to think what I'd say if the play were a flop. You're on Dave Garroway's show and he says to you, "Well, I see nobody liked your play." What do you say? I got up the next morning early to go on over. I hadn't quite taken in the night before what the various critics had said. I knew that Atkinson was favorable but not what he had said. Well, they put me in front of the lights, and they started by reading the Atkinson review. There were, oh, twelve seconds when I thought I was about to weep from coast to coast.

INTERVIEWER: How does it seem to be in the communal world of the theater, after the rather lonely discipline of writing verse?

MacLeish: I've done nothing but run into people and read books by people who, having stumbled innocently into the theater, later found themselves in a hell of a mess because the director was a son of a bitch or the producer was a son of a bitch or *all* the actors were sons of bitches. We had absolutely no difficulty. I had never met Kazan until we began to talk about his directing the play. We immediately became very close friends. He's a man inhabited by a demon, a real d-a-e-m-o-n. He's alive with a marvelous kind of creativity, not verbal, but tactile and of the eye and ear. He sees, he composes, *upon the stage.* He is a man of strong convictions, deep convictions, deep feelings, who understood entirely what the play was about, and what I was up to. De Liagre is another gift from God. I had never met him until he asked for the rights to the play after the Yale production. I was prepared to meet a successful producer (which he was) who would have little interest in poetry on the stage. Actually no author ever had a producer who cared more about his play. He had to care. His fellow producers were betting him he'd lose his shirt. But he never wavered—not even in Washington!

Well, de Liagre and I had never met. Kazan and I had never met. Kazan and de Liagre barely knew each other. Boris Aronson, wonderful man, great artist, knew none of us but Kazan. And when, later, we found David Amram to do the music—one of the most gifted composers for the stage in New York—he knew none of us and none of us knew him. The only one of the crew who knew most of the others was Lucinda Ballard, who did the costumes. Nevertheless this conglomeration of strangers somehow made a single mind, a single action. We had our differences—on one occasion over costumes. But the whole experience—and it was a *whole* experience—was a delight. Aronson's set, as I told him, made the play "possible." Kazan's direction made the possibility real. De Liagre was a part of everything that happened, and made the happening human. With the result that I look back with delight on what seems to be hell for more experienced playwrights—the particular delight which I had always thought of as peculiar to writing—to what they call "creation." Because this was creation—by

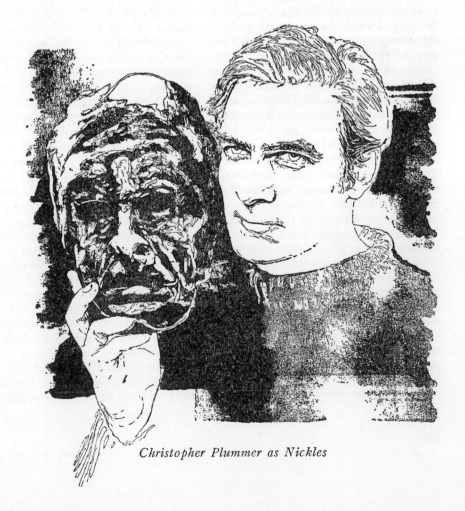

Christopher Plummer as Nickles

Raymond Massey as Mr. Zuss

all of them—and, what's more, by all of them *together*. I won't even try to talk about the actors. Except to say that the delight, of course, found its focus in them. To write words to be spoken on the stage and to find actors like those to speak them—well, you can imagine. Or perhaps you have to go through the whole thing to imagine it. In short, I liked the communal world of the theater, as you call it. In fact, that was what I liked best about it.

Because there was and is one aspect of the theater I don't like so well. I'm not talking about the so-called Broadway aspect of it. Actually the professional Broadway people understood this play a lot better than some of the professional intellectuals—much better. But what troubles me is that on the American stage as it is now established, a production costs so much money that the play has got to go on running for a long time, to get the money back. There is something about a long run, particularly with a play of this kind, which disturbs me. There it is. It's just something that's going on, unwinding itself, running along on its own clockwork, dutifully and devotedly watched by the producer and the director, served by the actors. It seems to be wrong as a system. I should think the repertory system, in which you put on a play, play it while it's new and exciting, and then take it off, would be a much more satisfactory one. But there's nothing you

can do about our system as long as it costs more than a hundred thousand dollars to put even a simple play with a simple set on the stage.

INTERVIEWER: In your own experience, you never found any commercial pressure to soften or dilute?

MACLEISH: No. This sort of thing would happen: the public relations people came around before we opened and said, "You know, it would be well if we didn't talk about this too much as a *verse* play, and if we didn't talk about it as a play on a Biblical theme, but talked about it as a play on a contemporary theme." Once we got going, the principal interest lay in the fact that it was a verse play on a Biblical theme. No, there was never any attempt to have words "softened" until we finally came around to the recording of the play. The RCA people were recording it, and after we talked about various other things, the fellow in charge said to me, very apologetically, "You know, our recordings are taken right into the family and played in the house. There are some words here that present some difficulties." He mentioned one.

"There are some others," I told him. But when we came to the end of it, only that one word was left out. And I don't blame them for that.

INTERVIEWER: Did you feel that any of the recommendations made in the course of the production applied to prose drama but

not to your play? Did you ever feel that the spectacle, for instance, was overwhelming the language?

MACLEISH: This is one place where I'd been warned by everybody that Kazan and I were going to have trouble, because Kazan is famous for his ability to dramatize visually and audibly, to such an extent that the action on stage carries you on its own back. He's done it again and again and again. And I'd been warned that he might do this to *J.B.* Something of the kind did seem at one point to be about to happen. He wanted to divide the disaster scenes from each other, to set them in frames: for example, he set the first one, the return of the soldiers, in the frame of the end of the war. He wanted brief little interscenes which would provide punctuation, and at one point those interscenes grew and grew until they really did get in the way. I wrote him a "note" about it. Gadg [Kazan] toned them down. And although some people think that they are too obtrusive now, I don't think they are. To me they serve their purpose. They are violent, but their very violence makes it possible for them to be extremely brief.

INTERVIEWER: Then Kazan accepted a recommendation of yours about the production. This was really a collaboration, a dialogue and not a monologue.

MACLEISH: Oh, yes. I never made a change in the text, either in the way of cutting, which is what I did largely, or in a few instances of rewriting, that I didn't want to make.

INTERVIEWER: Why did you change the age of Nickles?

MACLEISH: In the published book, Mr. Zuss and Nickles are both old men. It was Gadg who said, after he'd read the play four or five times, "Nickles is a young man. He talks like a young man. That's the way young beatniks talk. Life to him is disgusting, a miserable, horrible thing. He hates life. That's kid talk, not an old man's."

I said, "My eyes are opened."

INTERVIEWER: You don't feel that making the devil a young man takes away the authority of the antiquity of evil?

MACLEISH: Yes, there's a great deal to be said for letting evil have a little antiquity. Nickles is old in all the European productions. But there's also an awful lot to be said for the kind of passion of contempt that you can get out of a young man. After we decided to renew his youth, and after Chris Plummer, with this knowledge in mind, began reading the lines, I was astonished at the extent to which they began taking on edge.

INTERVIEWER: Many of Kazan's suggestions to you involve characters, their prominence and their relations with each other. Couldn't these suggestions be compared to those of a good editor in a publishing house when he reads a novel? How did his specifically theatrical intelligence help you?

MACLEISH: Because all of those suggestions came out of the effort to resolve *dramatic* problems, *theatrical* problems, *staging* problems. When I saw *J.B.* again after I got back from Antigua in April (I hadn't seen it for three months), I was absolutely overwhelmed by it. It seemed to me that as a spectacle on the stage, it was miraculous. This of course was Kazan. Then I realized that Kazan's great gift is the gift of the choreographer, his movement of people. He never wastes motion, doesn't rush the actors around the stage, but every motion is meaningful. There's an intricate and eloquent dance going on.

If you start with that conception of the way Gadg's mind works, you then come to the conclusion, which is absolutely sound, that his interest in the language of a play is really subordinate to his concern for the totality of the dramatic movement which is going to come to the dramatic conclusion. His concern with character (I thought about this a lot while he and I were talking; we really lived in each other's pockets for about six months) I could almost always trace to a concern with some unstated problem as to where he was going to *put* a man.

I don't mean to say for a moment that Gadg wasn't interested in the substance of the play, because he was, but he was interested first in the play as a realized *work* of art, as a tangible, sensible *thing*, out there on the stage with its noises and movements.

INTERVIEWER: I understand that it was in one of your walks around Washington that you and Kazan hit upon the final major revision, a change suggested to Kazan by Aristotle's "recognition scene." Could you tell us about this?

MACLEISH: Yes. There were things in the play that seemed to me on paper to work perfectly, but which when seen on the stage didn't. For example, a crucial point of the play is J.B.'s—Job's—response to God's voice out of the whirlwind. In the play as published, the nature of that response is dealt with in colloquy between Mr. Zuss and Nickles. Each one thinks he's been sold down the river. Nickles thinks that J.B. has surrendered, when he says, "Behold, I am vile . . . I will lay mine hand upon my mouth." Mr. Zuss thinks that J.B.'s repentance is false and forced and arrogant. And so, each one speaking against his own interest, they pass, like trains on parallel tracks. And they thus make clear—at least I hope they make clear—the ambiguity of J.B.'s conduct and J.B.'s words. On the stage, it became perfectly apparent that leaving the resolution of that all-important point to the conversation between these two observers isn't adequate.

Gadg and I walked around—this was a brisk, cold November morning—we walked around and around the park, and Gadg said, "How God-damned stupid can you be! How stupid can you be! All I've done is to take the recognition scene from this play and turn my principal actor, my protagonist, with his back to the audience. How stupid can you be!"

And I said, "Gadg, it's nice of you to put it that way, but the reason you put him with his back to the audience was that I hadn't given him a word to say. His presence there with his dumb face staring at the audience embarrassed you." And that was the fact. Now he meant by "the recognition scene" the point at which J.B. comes face to face with what he has sought, his vision of the ultimate, his vision of God. What he's been crying out to see, what he's heard about all his life, is suddenly there. And this voice tramples him into the clay, to use Yeats's phrase, and all that was happening at that point in the Washington production was that J.B. slowly got himself to his feet and stood, with his back to the audience, while Mr. Zuss and Nickles talked it out.

The moment Kazan had said what he

said, it became perfectly clear to both of us what had to be done. I was the one who had to do it. J.B. had to be put back into the center of the psychological action. The minute that happened the whole thing just fell into place.

INTERVIEWER: One last thing about the production: I know that Yeats, when he wrote plays in verse, felt that he had to instruct the actors of the Abbey Theatre in verse-speaking. In an article about the production of *J.B.*, it mentions that at the first meeting of the cast Kazan had you read the whole play aloud. Was this an endeavor to teach something about verse-speaking?

MACLEISH: I read it in a deliberate effort to establish cadence in the ears of people who weren't necessarily accustomed to hearing cadence. I could have spared myself the effort so far as Chris Plummer goes. Plummer has one of the most exquisite ears I've ever found anywhere, and he also has that gift which actors so rarely have of being willing to trust the lines to carry him; he will read the lines as the lines are, instead of trying to impose himself on them. Raymond Massey also has an extremely good ear. Hingle had never read verse before. He had to fight his tendency to try to get it back into prose. But he fought it beautifully. On the other hand, Jim Daly [James Daly, who replaced Hingle in the cast] is, I think, naturally sensitive to verse.

INTERVIEWER: I've been wondering about your earlier plays. *J.B.* is your seventh, by my count. You started with *Nobodaddy* and *Panic*, and then you did four radio plays, before coming to *J.B.* I wonder if you could take us through this list, and talk about your development as a dramatist.

MACLEISH: That's quite an order. I don't know if I can be very intelligent about it. I don't remember much about the writing of *Nobodaddy*. There's nothing very dramatic about it. Frankly, I remember little about it.

Panic I do remember quite well. As an editor of *Fortune*, I happened to be witnessing some of the more gruesome economic sights of the depression. I had my nose rubbed in them. I was also engaged at that time in a running war with the Marxists. Marxism was then the fashionable intellectual attitude. Almost everybody you knew was a Marxist writing on one paper or another. I don't mean that they were necessarily Communists, but they were very snotty and very superior and very much the little intellectuals, and they infuriated me as that attitude always has. I found myself warring with them particularly on the grave issues of determinism, economic necessity, and Marx's discovery of the ultimate laws of human society. *Panic* would be terribly dated now. The mark of its "timeliness" is the fact that it ran under its own steam for two nights, and it was fairly obvious that it wasn't going to be able to run a third night, but some Communist organization bought seats and kept it going for another night, on condition that I would appear after the performance and allow myself to be heckled by various dignitaries of the party. This all took place on the stage. I remember it with great vividness. I had a temperature of about 103 degrees and was feeling very little pain. The principal ground of attack was that I had made the Communist a blind man!

The radio plays, beginning with *The Fall of the City*, were exactly that. They were radio plays. I don't know why, but I became fascinated by the opportunity that radio offered for a staging that existed solely in the imagination. All you had to do was suggest a scene, and it would immediately be painted for the minds of your

listeners. You moved people on and off in any way you wanted to. And that possibility, plus an idea I carried over from my long poem *Conquistador*, made *The Fall of the City*. It was one of the old Aztec stories about what happened in Tenochtitlan before the Spaniards showed up: there were a series of prophecies, a dead woman coming out of her grave, prophesying, and I applied this idea to the coming of the Nazis in Austria and all its implications. It all fitted together, and provided a vehicle and a subject. I had not yet discovered a viable verse form, but the play has some verse that I think works. *Fall of the City* was done at least twice on a coast-to-coast network, and then it was done on local stations. And so that led naturally to another one, which was *Air Raid*, and which came out of the Spanish War. And *The Trojan Horse* is a further development, coming out of the McCarthy business. *This Music Crept by Me Upon the Waters* was an attempt to see whether it might not be pos-

sible to do a lyric play for radio. It's never been broadcast in the United States. It's been done a number of times by the BBC, but it's never been touched here.

INTERVIEWER: We were talking before about the actors' verse-speaking. I've wanted to ask you about the poetic line which you use in *J.B.* Have you worked, in your other plays, to find a type of poetic line which can be spoken on the modern stage?

MACLEISH: That, of course, is the interesting problem to me, too. There are some forewords in some of those early plays, *Panic*, I think, about a theory of mine which I dug up in the thirties. That the natural rhythm of English as spoken in America is trochaic, not iambic; falling from strong down instead of climbing from weak up. I think there's something in it—but not too much.

The real problem doesn't lie there. I was thinking then in terms of feet or measures, and I don't think that's the way you think about English verse. You really should think about it in terms of the line. In *J.B.* I did begin thinking about it in terms of the line and came to the conclusion, which I guess everybody else has come to, that the five-beat line just isn't in our American speech. It's not part of our language. We don't talk that way. We do however talk—or our talk can be crystallized, can be shaped—in a four-beat line.

What I was doing throughout a number of these plays was trying to find a four-beat line which, on the negative side, would not get muscle-bound and constricted, and which, on the positive side, would be capable of moving all the way from the most colloquial speech to the most lyrical. The four-beat line, of course, is traditionally a great lyric instrument in English poetry. I wanted to find a use of it—a form of it—which would enable me to have both.

Another reason why I wanted a definite four-beat line, instead of a line which might or might not have four beats, was that I came to the conclusion that in a verse play the *pattern* of the line is extremely important, that the listener must be *conscious* of the pattern of the line if it is to work. In other words I disagree with Tom Eliot's suggestion that the listener should only be aware of the pattern of the line at moments of great emotion or great stress. My feeling about that theory is that if you wait for those moments, then the pattern has to establish itself at that very moment, and instead of working out to enhance the emotion, it really works out to obstruct it.

No, I'm trying to find a pattern which can be heard movingly at a moment of stress, but which won't obtrude to destroy

Pat Hingle as J.B.

the more colloquial speech. I want a line which, having been once established, will be capable of putting itself, if you want it to do so, into hard lyric lines, or into softer lyric lines which nevertheless depend heavily upon the pattern of the line. That the lines should be heard *as* lines is what I've been trying to get at in *J.B.* And I do think that the line in *J.B.*, most of the time, does what I want it to do.

INTERVIEWER: While you've been writing all these plays, not to mention your poems, you've been doing so much else. You were an editor of *Fortune*, the Librarian of Congress, an Assistant Secretary of State, a founder of UNESCO, and goodness knows what else. Have these associations and activities been valuable to you as a writer?

MACLEISH: Let me break that down. First of all, I have never found any other activity that went together with writing verse. I tried law, which was perhaps the most *adventurous* mistake a man could make! I discovered that there was no possibility of practicing law the way I wanted to practice it, as a trial lawyer, and doing anything reflective. Journalism was no answer. The only way I was able to make anything out of a life that was supporting itself through journalism was to take pieces of the year off. God knows the government service, at least during the war, wasn't much help. As far as teaching goes, I've always felt that if I'd come to it as a youngster I would have found it just as difficult as the law or anything else.

That's one half of your question, the way in which the various things I've done or had to do throughout my life have related to being a writer of verse. The answer is that they related badly, all of them. I don't know any solution and I don't think there is any solution. It's like the American people looking for security in the present world.

The other aspect of this question is the fruitfulness of these various things, as they have turned up later in my writing. The law theoretically ought to have been very fruitful, because my career as a practicing lawyer, though brief, was nevertheless hectic. It was full of trial cases. I owe the training a great deal, but I don't think I've ever gone back to actual material, the cases. Journalism, the kind of journalism I engaged in as an editor of *Fortune* during the depression, was a different kettle of fish altogether. It was full of useful things. I had to make up my mind, in the early thirties, about a lot of questions which I wouldn't have considered if I had gone on writing in isolation. For example, I had to make up my mind throughout the course of one year

about the state of housing in America. It sounds like a dull subject, but believe me it isn't. And I found myself writing articles on inflation and the politics of the Japanese empire, three or four years before the war. All of these things have tended to be extremely fruitful. They have come back to me again and again. *Panic* came straight out of the journalistic experience. So far as government service goes, the chief increment of public service, in the way in which I knew it—as Assistant Secretary of State and as Librarian of Congress and as a minor associate of Mr. Roosevelt—is a kind of knowledge of human nature and conduct that you don't get otherwise and otherwhere. And I can't think of anything more useful for a poet than that. So far as teaching goes, there the riches are enormous, particularly when you come back at it late, when you find yourself forced to reread, re-examine, reconclude, and all of it in relation not to your own mind and your own needs, but to the minds and needs of other people.

INTERVIEWER: Then I gather you don't regret the time you have spent not writing.

MACLEISH: I don't regret the time I've spent not writing. Actually, it seems to me I've gotten more writing done than I really should have. I've written a *hell* of a lot of prose. I'm just shocked to see how much prose I've written. It's mostly in the form of essays and speeches, largely on political subjects, very rarely on literary ones. This is on my mind right now because we're about to put together a sort of all-inclusive volume of my prose. So far as the verse goes, I have really written more verse than I should have. I think it would have been better if there hadn't been so much of it. There's a distinct limit to the amount of time you ought to try to spend on actual writing. If you try to spend too much, the result is frustration and paralysis. I dare say we all know young men who were blessed by God with a large independent income and no obligations of any kind, who had nothing to do but write, and who very shortly stopped writing. They just couldn't take it. They had nothing else to do. As Ernest Hemingway used to say, "Writing isn't a full-time profession"; and it isn't. That is, not our kind of writing—the kind of writing that you spin out of yourself. We're not mechanical spiders, we're spiders that have to produce our own fluff *from* somewhere.

INTERVIEWER: Let me bring up another thing I've been wondering about. What did

Nan Martin as Sarah

you think of *J.B.*'s audience at the ANTA Theatre? Were they understanding the play? Were they there for fashion? How many people in the New York audience can a poet count on to see his serious play seriously?

MACLEISH: That's a hell of a question. There was a time when, after the play had been going for about two months, de Liagre told me that he was holding his left ear lobe all the time because he was perfectly convinced there was a limited highbrow audience and we must have run through it. But we didn't run through it. What one noticed about the people there was that they were not the people you expected to see in a Broadway audience. They looked different. I would guess from my mail, which has been voluminous, that we got a great many people who were there because the theme concerned them deeply.

INTERVIEWER: I guess I've been thinking about an audience in general. The public for modern poetry is tiny, and you are a modern poet. Many people seem to feel it is the audience that has defected from poetry, and not the poets from their audience. Does the popularity of *J.B.* ever give you qualms? If the audience is debased, is the popular work of art necessarily debased?

MacLeish: One of my colleagues at Harvard said to a mutual friend, speaking of *J.B.*, "You know I think I would have liked it if it hadn't been a success." No, it doesn't trouble me, nor do I think I ought to be troubled by it. What I'm troubled by is the reverse of it. I'm troubled by the extent to which, not contemporary poetry, but criticism of contemporary poetry (and the kind of vehicle in which criticism of contemporary poetry is most often found) tends to make a virtue of the smallness of audience. I mean, the attitude that if a book of verse or a poet in the totality of his work or a particular poem has a general human appeal, there must necessarily be something meretricious and cheap about it. This is a kind of artistic onanism, isn't it?

INTERVIEWER: I am interested that most of the hostile criticism of *J.B.* seems to have been ideological, rather than dramatic.

MacLeish: Yes, I think that's a hopeful thing. I think it's hopeful that you can get people in America in this generation to feel violently about ideas in a verse play. One angry lady complained that *J.B.* isn't a play about "the condition of man" *today*. She should read my mail.

INTERVIEWER: We haven't really talked much about ideology. What has interested you in the discussions of the play's ideas?

MacLeish: One thing is the relation of Nickles to the existential point of view. There's a rather interesting paradox, from my point of view, in that whereas Nickles sounds a good deal like an uninformed disciple of Sartre who has picked up a purely negative existentialism, the play itself—the line of the play and the conclusion of the play—are quite existential in another way, the way in which Paul Tillich is existential. Tillich's conception of the human situation, and of the kind of affirmation of life a man makes simply by living it, is very close to the way my mind goes, and very close to the direction of *J.B.* I've seen *J.B.* called an existential play, and I've also seen it called an anti-existential play. I think both remarks could be made: in relation to Nickles, and in relation to the play as a whole.

You can't really tell from a man's church what he's going to say about *J.B.* Some of the Catholic comments on the play have been pretty savage. On the other hand some of the most enthusiastic reviews I've seen have been Catholic. Not only in Italy, where there were a number, but in this country, too. I think it depends, very largely, on the extent to which the particular Catholic is able to deal with the religious

problem as distinguished from the problem of dogma. If you take *J.B.* in terms of dogma, of course it becomes intensely heretical. On the other hand, if you take it in terms of the human experience, it would seem to me to be a religious play if I understand what the word religious means. By that I don't mean that it's on a religious subject. I mean that it moves through a human experience and comes to a conclusion which is only acceptable in terms of belief—the belief in life—not in terms of reason, any more than in terms of dogma.

This debate touches the essentials of the play. Whether or not one thinks that I've been fair to psychiatry, or whether or not one thinks my Communist is a fair example of Communist thinking, these are things of minor importance compared to the question whether the *experience* with which the play tries to deal is a real human experience, whether people do live through it or can live through it pretty much in the way in which it is lived through in the play, and whether the solution is "conceivable."

INTERVIEWER: Some Biblical scholars complain that the beginning and end of Job are later emendations, don't they?

MacLeish: It seems really rather infantile to protest against the beginning and the end of the Book of Job as being unworthy of God. This happens to be the way God does move on occasion. That's what happens in the world.

INTERVIEWER: I have a question that's not related to anything we've said, but that interests me. Eliot has said that writing his plays influenced a change of style in his poems. A change of diction widened the possible audience for his later poems, and he thinks that writing plays contributed to the change. I wonder if you feel that writing *J.B.* will affect the poems you write.

MacLeish: Actually, what I think I will be doing from now on out is to write verse for the stage. I haven't been writing lyrics at all. You see I've been doing nothing but *J.B.* for three or four years. Now I've started right back on another play. This is what I want to do. It's more exciting to me, more inviting.

INTERVIEWER: Can you tell us about the new play?

MacLeish: I can only say this, that this is a play which bears much the same relation to the myth of Herakles that *J.B.* bears to the Book of Job.

INTERVIEWER: Let me ask you another. You described your experience with *J.B.* as educational. What advice could you give, spreading your education, to a poet who wanted to write verse for the stage?

MacLeish: If he could possibly have in

some way the experience that I've had, it'd be the happiest thing of all. For a youngster who has to find his way, it would be perhaps somewhat difficult, but it's by no means impossible. One of the things that I hope we're going to do in the new theater at Harvard is to find means of inviting a topnotch director to come to Cambridge perhaps twice during the year to mount a play that he wanted to mount, and that people in Cambridge wanted to do, to see; he would use the actors we have, the designers we have, and go through the whole painful, exciting, agonizing business of getting a play on the stage. I can't think of anything that would teach a young playwright more than to go through that sort of experience.

INTERVIEWER: What do you think is the major problem facing the poetic dramatist now? Is it the money required to stage a play on Broadway?

MacLeish: No, I don't think that's the problem. I would think that if a play like *J.B.* can be done—which is to say a verse play on a tragic theme by a man who had no reputation whatever as a playwright—there is no reason to suppose that the doors are closed to a particular *kind* of play in a particular *kind* of medium. I think the real problem is a problem that quite a number of poets are working at: the problem of finding a dramatic form *and* verse form—a dramatic form appropriate to verse, a verse form appropriate to drama. Both forms must be appropriate to the kind of experience and the kind of sensibility which we think of as modern. That doesn't necessarily mean modern in terms of theme. A play can be *about* now without *being* now.

There's a whole problem there which nobody has really yet solved, but which must be soluble. The solution would promise very great, if immaterial, rewards. You'd be astonished at the number of people whom you would not think of as having any particular interest in poetry, the number of people on Broadway, as a matter of fact, who are intensely and deeply and passionately interested in getting poetry back on the stage. Not for chichi reasons, reasons of being "cultivated" or anything of that kind, but for real reasons. It's something—not just poetry on the stage, but a poetry adapted to the modern stage—that I think a great many people are eagerly waiting for, hoping for. And I have a feeling there is a generation of young writers coming along which will give it to them.

Donald Hall has published two books of verse, Exiles and Marriages *(the 1955 Lamont Poetry Selection) and* The Dark Houses. *He is at present living in England.*

THE EDUCATION OF
RENAISSANCE
MAN

In his pioneer school in Mantua, Vittorino da Feltre

taught classical learning and bodily graces and bred

a line of enlightened princes and patrons who sought

to embody his ardent ideal of the "complete citizen"

Some of the intellectual rigor of Humanist education is suggested by Vincenzo Foppa's fresco of a very youthful scholar reading Cicero (whose initials M. T. C. appear on the bench behind).

By IRIS ORIGO

Under Vittorino da Feltre's guidance Ludovico Gonzaga, Marquis of Mantua, had acquired the taste and wisdom that made him one of the great princes of Italy. In this Mantegna fresco he is seated at left, speaking to a secretary. Between him and his wife are their two youngest children, and behind them two older sons: Federigo and Gianfrancesco. The fresh-faced young woman at right center is Federigo's wife. The others are courtiers.

In the little dominion of Mantua, in the year 1423, an experiment in education began, of which the results were more far-reaching than its founder could ever, in his most hopeful moments, have foreseen. His name was Vittorino da Feltre, and his school was called La Giocosa. The pupils schooled there, and later on their children and grandchildren, grew up to form little centers of civilization as complete as the world has ever seen—the courts of Mantua and Urbino, of Ferrara and Milan—and the ideas underlying that civilization are still under active debate today. After five hundred years, the famous "Renaissance Man" still seems rather larger than life-size—not only a scholar but an athlete, a captain of armies, a wise ruler, and a patron of all the arts. Were these claims indeed justified? If they were, it is surely still pertinent to inquire by what process it was that such a man was shaped.

Let us look first at the man who founded this school and directed it for twenty-three years: Vittorino Rambaldoni, generally known, from his little native city in the Venetian Alps, as Vittorino da Feltre. His appearance, according to the two portraits remaining of him and the accounts of his contemporaries, was unimpressive—a man small and slight in stature, with an ascetic yet kindly face, a quiet voice, and a gentle and unemphatic manner, who was always dressed in a plain dark scholar's gown and rough sandals. Yet so high was this little schoolmaster's reputation that when, on a visit to Pope Eugenius IV, he knelt at the Pontiff's feet, the Pope raised him up, exclaiming, "How great a soul is lodged in this little body! Had my position allowed it, it is I who would have liked to rise, as he came in."

When Gianfrancesco Gonzaga, Marquis of Mantua, invited Vittorino to his court as preceptor to his sons, the teacher—who had had schools of his own in Padua and Venice—hesitated greatly before accepting, and then did so on two conditions: that his employer should never require anything of him "unworthy of either of us," and that, in the management of the boys and the household, he should be given as free a hand "as if he were the boys' own father." Gianfrancesco agreed; and

Medal of Vittorino da Feltre by Pisanello

Vittorino, without even inquiring what his salary was to be, took up his new post.

The house which was assigned to him and his pupils was a fine villa on the outskirts of Mantua. Built in 1388 by Gianfrancesco's predecessor as a pleasure house, it stood in the midst of wide meadows sloping down to the river Mincio and was bordered by broad, shady avenues, while the interior was decorated with frescoes of beasts, birds, and children at play. Vittorino started by stripping it of every luxury: fine hangings and draperies, silver and gold plates and ornaments. Then he turned to the daily life of his pupils. The young Gonzagas—of whom the two elder, Ludovico and Carlo, at once came into his charge, the younger children later on— were not at first sight prepossessing pupils. Ludovico was a fat, phlegmatic boy with a great belly and dragging steps, who spent his days in eating, drinking, and sleeping; Carlo, while tall and active, was rickety and nervous. (Both boys were soon restored to health by their preceptor's wise diet.) Their companions, the sons of the Mantuan nobles, were a set of spoiled and lawless boys dressed in fine silks and brocades adorned with jewels, heavily scented and pomaded, who came to school whenever they pleased and spent much of their time there with acrobats and jesters.

To all this Vittorino swiftly put an end. After a short period of patient inaction, during which he quietly observed each pupil, he firmly dismissed a few whom he considered incorrigible, and those servants who had encouraged their bad habits. He placed a reliable porter at the gate, so that no one could come in or go out without his permission. He obtained the Marquis' permission to summon a few of his former pupils from Venice, to appoint competent teachers for every branch of learning, and to award scholarships to some poor boys of outstanding gifts, who were received at La Giocosa (as they had been in his previous school in Padua) "for the love of God." Then he set to work.

The object of his training was, in his own words, the full development of each of the principal elements of man's nature: "the mind, the body, and the heart." The first two parts of this formula were, of course, based on the familiar Platonic principle: "gymnastic for the body and music for the mind." The rest of it was based on the teachings of Christianity. And it was the combination of both, the harmonious blending of the ideals of Humanism and of Christianity, which gave to Vittorino's school its particular flavor.

In returning to the classical conception of the equal development of body and mind, Vittorino swept aside many centuries of medieval prejudice, according to which the body represented only the lower part of our nature. It is true that at the medieval courts young knights had been taught to ride, joust, and hunt, but never had it been admitted that, as Plato had taught, the perfect man could only be formed by a harmonious balance between mind and body. But now Vittorino turned La Giocosa into a true classical gymnasium. His pupils were taught to run, to wrestle, to play football, to hunt, to swim and fish in the waters of the Mincio, and to learn the arts of javelin-throwing, archery, and dancing. In summer they were even taken mountain-climbing (then a most unusual pursuit) in the Venetian Alps. And so much attention was paid to dignity of carriage that if Vittorino saw a boy standing about awkwardly or slouching, he would chalk a circle around the place where the boy stood and require him to remain there motionless for a specified time, in the presence of his companions in a correct posture.

All the sports of La Giocosa must have made the school a paradise for active boys, compared to the almost wholly sedentary lives of the pupils of the monastic orders, but for Vittorino their real purpose was training in hardihood and self-restraint. Just as he abolished any corporal punishment, so he required his pupils to show their own respect for their

matics, and, with some reservations, music and dancing. Indeed the only major subjects excluded were medicine, theology, and the law, which were university subjects in any case. Vittorino, however, always maintained that it was not fair to expect every pupil to show the same tastes and talents. "Whatever our own predilections may be, we recognize that we must follow nature's lead." He declared that "everyone has some gift, if only one can discover it," and he therefore bestowed especial pains upon the dullest boys, trying to find some subject or skill to meet their needs.

Such individual attention was all the more remarkable when we consider that his school contained sixty or seventy pupils of the most various ages (the Gonzaga children entered at the age of five, but Sassuolo da Prato only at twenty-one). We are told that—in the belief that five hours of sleep were enough for a keen scholar—Vittorino would walk about the school in the dark on early winter mornings with a candle in one hand and a book in the other, rousing the ablest scholars from their sleep, to work with them for an extra hour, "and encourage them with grave and earnest words to high endeavor."

The youngest children learned to read by playing games with colored letter cards. Arithmetic, too, was at first taught as a game; for, like Quintilian, Vittorino believed that "the first thing to be avoided is, that a child should begin by feeling aversion for the studies he cannot yet love." History and mythology, too, were told as exciting and ennobling stories. By the time the child was six or seven he was ready to begin his serious studies in *grammatica*, the foundation of all knowledge, for this word comprised not only the study of Greek and Latin grammar (both languages being started together) but the reading of the great classical authors. A great deal of the teaching was oral: in the grammar lesson the master would dictate the list of words to be learned by heart and their declensions, commenting on any grammatical difficulty as it arose. When the time came for reading the Greek or Latin text itself, the master would first read a passage aloud, explaining and commenting, followed by each pupil reading the same passage in turn, until not only his translation but his

bodies by the greatest moderation in eating, drinking, and sleeping; by regular exercise in all seasons; and by denying themselves any self-indulgence, such as wearing gloves or furs or fine linen or sleeping in featherbeds, or even allowing themselves a small fire on the coldest, most misty days of the Mantuan winter. "Clap your hands or stamp your feet," he would say to his boys when they were cold, "or say a fine poem, to stir the sluggish blood in your veins." He himself, even when visibly numb with cold, was never seen to stand before a fire.

So much for one side of education at La Giocosa. What was the academic training? Vergerius, who taught in the University of Padua when Vittorino was there, defined "liberal studies" as "those worthy of being studied by free men, to promote virtue and knowledge." The approved subjects included first, of course, the classics; then philosophy and history, mathe-

enunciation and expression were considered perfect. Finally each passage was learned by heart. Every child was taught to read aloud agreeably and clearly, "not muttering in his teeth," and without uncouth gestures or making faces. And Vittorino was always especially pleased when any of them asked questions, saying that a passive acceptance of instruction was an infallible sign of an inattentive, dull, or lazy mind.

In the choice of authors, the principle was that laid down by Vergerius: "Begin with the best." Virgil, Homer, Cicero, and Demosthenes were the four authors on whom the teaching at La Giocosa was based. Only after these had been thoroughly mastered were the pupils allowed to pass on to Lucan and Ovid (in extracts, to "form an elegiac taste"), as well as to Xenophon and Herodotus. Terence, Plautus, Horace, and Juvenal were permitted only to the older boys, whose characters were considered to be already formed. In Greek the advanced students were allowed to read first Aeschylus and then Euripides and Sophocles, as well as Pindar, Theocritus, and some parts of Aristophanes. Vittorino thought it very important to learn Greek at the same time as Latin, and, since he considered himself only a mediocre Greek scholar, he engaged two renowned Greek teachers for La Giocosa, both recommended by the great Humanist Francesco Filelfo—George of Trebizond and the celebrated grammarian Theodore Gaza.

All the pupils were expected to write Greek and Latin verses and to compose speeches in these languages, which they recited to their companions or to distinguished guests. One boy composed such an oration to thank his fellow students for having saved him from drowning. Gianlucido Gonzaga, at fourteen, recited two hundred Latin hexameters of his own composition, celebrating the arrival of the Emperor Sigismund in Mantua, to an illustrious visitor, the Abbot Ambrogio of Camaldoli, "with so much grace," according to his hearer, "that I think Virgil spoke no better when he recited the sixth book of the *Aeneid* to Augustus." And he added that on the same day Gianlucido's sister of ten, Cecilia, wrote for him in Greek and Latin "with so much elegance as to put me to shame, considering that among my own pupils I could scarcely find one capable of doing the same." In these orations Vittorino advised his pupils to use a clear, straightforward style, avoiding archaisms and any excessive display of learning; and indeed it is plain that he was well aware of the dangers, as well as the advantages, of too great a skill in rhetoric. "There is," he said, "nothing that may eventually do greater harm to a city than eloquence, for . . . when it is possessed by evil men, they may use it to stir up trouble and to corrupt public manners."

As for the other subjects, history was confined to that of Greece and Rome, ignoring both medieval and contemporary history, and was entirely uncritical. Vittorino, for instance, whose favorite historian was Livy, indignantly repudiated any suggestion that so great a man could ever have been inaccurate. Equally, the study of philosophy was limited to

ethics—that is, to the study of precepts from Cicero, Aristotle, Seneca, and Boethius, with illustrations from Plutarch, and at La Giocosa (though not in most other schools), of some of the Fathers of the Church, particularly Saint Jerome. Mathematics was given an important place and included geometry and astronomy. Vittorino also added the study of natural history (in a very rudimentary form) but discarded and despised astrology, in spite of its general popularity. As to music, many Humanists still regarded it, as the Middle Ages had done, with a considerable amount of distrust, declaring that too many young men "lose all vigor of mind and of character in their absorption in unworthy harmonies." But Vittorino, like Plato, held that it was necessary to the formation of a "complete" man; at La Giocosa both singing and playing the lyre and the lute were taught, and even dancing to music was approved.

In this connection a word must be said—since it was in this, too, that Humanist education broke new ground—about Vittorino's views on the education of women. His only girl pupils were the two Gonzaga daughters, Cecilia and Margherita, but other little bluestockings were being formed at much the same time in other parts of Italy. In Verona, Guarino's two pupils, Isotta and Ginevra Nogarola, were given a sound classical education. In Florence, when Poliziano fell in love with his beautiful pupil Alessandra Scala, it was in Greek verses that they corresponded. "You bring me, Alessandra, sweet violets—but I would taste the fruit."

There are, however, several prevalent misconceptions about the Humanist education of women. The first is that up to that time no girls had received any education at all: little Minervas, learned and wise, had sprung full-armed from the brains of Vittorino, Guarino, or Poliziano. Yet there is, for instance, the description given by the Tuscan chronicler Giovanni Morelli of his sister Mea, a whole century before the emergence of the young ladies of the Renaissance. This young lady, who had "hands of ivory, so well-shaped that they seemed to have been drawn by Giotto," was "delicate and pleasant in her speech, modest and measured in her gestures, yet a valiant, frank woman with a virile soul. She read and wrote as well as any man, she danced and sang perfectly, she was skilled in the arts of housekeeping, guiding her family with good advice and good habits, and living cheerfully and

No one owed more to Vittorino's inspired teaching than Federigo da Montefeltro, Duke of Urbino and among the most cultivated of Renaissance princes. This portrait—possibly by Justus van Ghent, more probably by Pedro Berruguete—shows him reading to his son Guidobaldo. On his left leg the Duke wears the Order of the Garter, awarded him by Edward IV of England. The richly dressed boy, about five years of age, is holding his father's sceptre.

gaily." This is, surely, a woman as highly civilized (except for a knowledge of Latin and Greek) as any daughter of the Renaissance. Moreover, it is also not entirely true that Vittorino, or indeed any other Humanist, advocated the *same* education for girls as for their brothers. Cecilia and Margherita Gonzaga did indeed study the classics. They were encouraged to know something of history, to practice the arts of agreeable conversation, to ride and dance and sing and play the lute, and above all, to appreciate poetry; since, according to the first treatise on education dedicated to a woman (written by Leonardo Bruni for Battista Malatesta), "anyone ignorant of and indifferent to so valuable an aid to knowledge and so ennobling a source of pleasure can by no means be entitled to be called educated." But arithmetic and geometry were wholly omitted from their curriculum, and also rhetoric, as "absolutely outside a woman's province." And the *first* place in a woman's education (in this all teachers agreed) was to be given to "the whole field of religion and morals, as a subject peculiarly her own."

And now we come to the third and most important part of Vittorino's method: the formation of what he called "the heart" and we should call character. Since he well knew that it can be formed only by example, he spent every hour of the day with his pupils, bearing a silent witness by his own life to the virtues he most valued: self-restraint, modesty, truthfulness, and kindness. His gentle equanimity, we are told, was the result of a stern self-discipline, by which he had conquered the sensuality and quick temper of his youth—at La Giocosa he led a life as dedicated as any monk's. His generosity was as spontaneous as his gentle smile: not only did many penniless students owe him their education, but his purse was always open to the poor. At his death, in spite of the handsome yearly salary of 240 gold florins awarded him by the Gonzagas, it was found that there was nothing left for his heirs but a little farm not far from Mantua, on the very site (and this must have delighted him) which was believed to be that of Virgil's birthplace. He was generous, too, with what he valued more than money: his fine collection of books, lending them freely, but becoming so angry when they were taken without leave that a law was passed in Mantua declaring the unauthorized borrowing of a book to be a punishable misdemeanor, like any other theft.

A poet in his youth, he finally destroyed the few poems he had kept and wrote very little else; all his energy went into his studies and his teaching. A devout Christian, he never required of his boys an austerity equal to his own (he lived on the most frugal of diets and scourged himself daily), but he did demand a daily attendance at Mass, confession once a month, and, above all, a deep reverence in word and deed. The only occasion when, breaking his own rule, he inflicted a corporal punishment was when he overheard Carlo Gonzaga blaspheme in the heat of a quarrel, and gave him, in the presence of the whole school, a sound box on the ear.

But the punishment that his pupils most dreaded was merely his displeasure and, in cases of cruelty or deceit, his glance of contempt and refusal to speak for several days to the offender. This was the more marked because at all other times his relationship with the boys was easy and affectionate, sharing their sports, delighting in their successes. Abbot Ambrogio has left us a charming description of him at the Gonzaga castle of Goito in the hills, where he had taken some of his younger pupils to escape from the summer heat: the children clustering round "on the happiest terms with him" to take part in the talk and show off their accomplishments, and then, when the guest left, riding with him for some distance to speed him on his way.

It should always be remembered that Vittorino considered Humanist education to be, above all, a *practical* preparation for life. His aim, he said, was not the formation of a great scholar but of a complete citizen. "Not everyone is obliged to excel in philosophy, medicine, or the law, nor are all equally favored by nature; but all are destined to live in society and to practice virtue." (By society he meant, of course, not only the world of the courts, but the community of men.) It was for this reason that, in spite of his personal interest in the clever poor students whom he himself had brought to the school, he attached an especial importance to the training of young noblemen, realizing that it was they who would become the model for all their subjects. It is in this sense only that La Giocosa can be considered, like the public schools of England, a school for the formation of a ruling class. But it was certainly, in its emphasis on the fusion of virtue and knowledge, a school for an elite—in Vergerius' words, for "free men."

And now we may inquire, what indeed were the fruits of this education? The Milky Way that led from La Giocosa across the skies of the Renaissance is full of minor stars: grammarians and versifiers, mathematicians, learned bishops, a musician and a *condottiere*. But we know that the formation of able scholars, or indeed of specialists of any kind, was not Vittorino's purpose. Did he then succeed in his ultimate aim, that of forming some "complete" human beings? The answer is, I think, both yes and no. The moral climate of the courts was a very different one from that inculcated on the playing fields of La Giocosa, and the violence, cruelty, and treachery which underlay the civilization of the Renaissance inevitably tainted the lives and characters of many of his pupils—except those who, like the brilliant and gentle Cecilia Gonzaga, forsook the life of the world for a convent. The rest had to deal with the society of their time as they found it—a world in which their old master's lessons of truthfulness, mildness, and forbearance held little place. Where Vittorino was entirely successful, however, was in the transmission of a certain fineness of *taste*—in life as well as in art. Ferrara under Lionello d'Este and his bride Margherita Gonzaga; Mantua under Ludovico Gonzaga and his son Federigo, and again in

Guidobaldo da Montefeltro, Federigo's sensitive and scholarly son (upper left), married Elisabetta Gonzaga (above), the gentle granddaughter of Ludovico of Mantua. Together they presided over the court of Urbino, which attracted the best artists and scholars in Italy. Among them were Baldassare Castiglione (left), who described the life at Urbino in one of the most delightful books of the Renaissance, The Courtier *(for an excerpt, see page 73). In it, Castiglione set up his model of what Chaucer would have called "a verray parfit gentle knight," Lord Chesterfield a gentleman, and still later generations a man of the world. Vittoria Colonna wrote to him, "I do not wonder that you have depicted the perfect courtier, for you had only to hold a mirror before you, and set down what you saw there." The attribution of Guidobaldo's portrait is uncertain; Castiglione's is by Raphael, and Elisabetta's probably by Montegna.*

the next generation, under Federigo's son Francesco, who brought home Isabella d'Este as his bride; Urbino under Federigo da Montefeltro and his son Guidobaldo, who married Ludovico Gonzaga's granddaughter Elisabetta; and finally, Milan under the rule of Beatrice d'Este (Isabella's sister) and her husband Ludovico Sforza—these four courts showed, under the influence of Vittorino's pupils or their descendants, a remarkably fine flowering of the human spirit, an exquisite pattern of civilized life. If their members did not all, in Vittorino's sense, "practice virtue," they certainly had learned to perfection how "to live in society." Indeed, all other societies before and since, with perhaps the exception of eleventh-century Japan, seem by comparison a little graceless, a little coarse.

Two men, both pupils of Vittorino's, stand out as the dominating figures of two of these courts: Ludovico Gonzaga, Marquis of Mantua, and Federigo da Montefeltro, Duke of Urbino. Both were skillful and intrepid *condottieri;* both were also wise rulers; both made their courts centers of learning and of the arts.

The temperaments of these two men, however, were widely dissimilar. From early youth Federigo (in spite of his illegitimate birth) had seemed marked for success. *"Tu quoque Caesar eris"* (You also will be Caesar), Vittorino would remind him in his school days, and it is said that his pupil's promise sometimes caused him to shed tears of joy. Ludovico, on the other hand, had so many obstacles to overcome that one may doubt whether he would ever have become a great man without the early help of his master. It was Vittorino's training that, in his boyhood, enabled him to conquer his ill-health and his tendency to corpulence and apathy; and it was also Vittorino's intercession that at last obtained his father's forgiveness when, having despaired of ever being able to rival his handsome, gifted younger brother Carlo at home, he took service under Filippo Maria Visconti in Milan and spent long, bitter years abroad in exile. Yet it may well have been these years spent earning his spurs as a *condottiere* that fortified and matured him, for when he inherited the state of Mantua, Ludovico at once showed himself a wise and provident ruler. He built dikes and banks to stem the floods of the river Po and a canal (designed by Brunelleschi) to irrigate the Mantuan plain, assigning the land to anyone who was prepared to farm it properly; he paved the city streets, built a hospital, and set up a printing press. He summoned the great architect Alberti to design two new churches, that of San Sebastiano and the Basilica of Sant' Andrea; the mathematician Bartolomeo Manfredi to make the clock for his great new belfry; and Andrea Mantegna to decorate his palace, declaring that Mantegna's little toe was dearer to him than the whole body of most of his subjects.

Under Vittorino's guidance Ludovico enriched his library with rare manuscripts. (It included not only a fine collection of Greek and Latin authors and of medieval manuscripts, but a few books in the Vulgar, among them one thus described in the inventory: "INCIPIT, *nel mezo del camin di nostra vita,* ET FINIT, *l'amor che move il sole e l'altre stelle,"* CONTINET CARTAS 74.) He seized every pretext—a birth or a wedding or a foreign prince's visit—for great feasts and banquets; he offered constant hospitality to scholars such as Filelfo and Pico della Mirandola, and such poets as Poliziano, whose *Orpheus* was written and performed in Mantua. And if at the end of all this the Mantuan coffers were empty, he was not ashamed to ask one of his artists to wait a little longer for full payment, since, he said, at the moment the Gonzaga jewels were in pawn! Yet the portraits of him that have come down to us are not those of a happy man. They show the face of a ruler who has achieved power and security, but on whom the years of struggle and anxiety have left their mark—a man always on his guard, never forgetful of the motto on the family crest, CAUTIUS, "live cautiously."

It is to the other of Vittorino's most famous pupils, Federigo da Montefeltro, that we must turn to see not only the qualities of the mind, but also of the heart, that La Giocosa sought to form; for here indeed we are close to finding Vittorino's "complete man." Although he was not entirely free, as a *condottiere,* from the cruelty of other soldiers of fortune, Federigo was almost unique in his faithfulness to his word and to his friends, in defeat as in victory. As a ruler his generosity and friendliness, and a total absence of the suspicion and arrogance of almost all other princes of his times, endeared him to all his subjects. Accounts by his contemporaries describe him as spending a part of each day, alone and unguarded, in the market place or in the shops of his artisans. "To one he would say, 'How is your old father?' to another, 'How does your trade thrive?' or 'Have you got a wife yet?' . . . One he took by the hand, he put his hand on another's shoulder, and spoke to all uncovered, so that men would say, when anyone was very busy, 'Why, you have more to do than Federigo's berretta!' "

One morning, meeting a wedding procession, Federigo dismounted to join the escort that was honoring the bride; and on a winter's day, when the monastery of San Bernardino, outside the city, was snowed in, he himself set off at the head of his men to cut a path through the snow to feed the hungry monks. In times of famine he distributed corn free from his private estate in Apulia. Whenever possible, he answered petitions on the same day he received them. It is hardly surprising that, as he walked through the streets, people would kneel down, crying, "God keep you, *signore!"*

At the same time Federigo displayed to the full, with the fruits of his successful wars, the magnificence expected of a Renaissance prince. Life in the great palace designed for him by Laurana was on a truly royal scale. His household counted "500 mouths," which included—besides knights, men-at-arms, grooms, and servants—four teachers of grammar, philosophy, and rhetoric, five architects and engineers, a German

The Gonzagas maintained the intellectual and artistic splendor of Mantua through the reigns of Ludovico, his son Federigo, and his grandson Francesco. The latter brought home a dazzling wife, Isabella d'Este, who surrounded herself with writers, architects, and painters. Among the works she commissioned is the curious picture above, one of five "allegories" she ordered for the decoration of her private apartments in the Gonzaga palace. Lorenzo Costa painted it according to her precise instructions, which included the peremptory order: "It is forbidden to you to add anything whatever of your own." It has been given various titles and interpretations over the centuries, for the allegory is anything but clear. It probably glorifies the triumph of poetry and music, and it is likely that Isabella herself is the lady being crowned with laurel by a cherub. These were the imaginary realms into which this brilliant, grasping woman, who wished to see and to learn and to possess everything, escaped —a retreat from the cruelty and intrigue around her into an ideal world of "luxe, calme, et volupté."

67

astrologer, five "readers aloud at meals," four "elderly and staid gentlemen" for his wife's court, four transcribers of manuscripts, the keeper of the bloodhounds, and the keeper of the giraffe. His stables held three hundred horses; his library, the rarest and most complete collection of manuscripts and books in Europe. His own tastes remained those formed at La Giocosa. Livy and Saint Augustine were read aloud to him at meals, and in the afternoons, if he was not watching a joust or some boys practicing gymnastics on the wide meadow of San Francesco, he would attend a classical lecture, or discuss theology, through a grating, with the learned Abbess of the Convent of Santa Chiara.

His son Guidobaldo followed in his father's footsteps. At a very early age he showed a passion for the classics and for geography and history, as well as for the gymnastics and knightly sports which greatly injured his already fragile health. After his marriage at sixteen to Ludovico Gonzaga's granddaughter Elisabetta, their court became a magnet for the best scholars and artists in Italy. The scholar Pietro Bembo came for a few days' visit, and stayed for six years; Castiglione came and wrote *Il Cortigiano*. The artists at Guidobaldo's court were Piero della Francesca, Francesco di Giorgio, Justus van Ghent, Ambrogio da Milano, Giovanni Sanzi (who was also the court chronicler), and above all, Sanzi's son, "the divine Raphael," who later on, in his famous *School of Athens* in the Vatican, reproduced the very quintessence of the Renaissance view of the classical world.

The days were spent in hunting, jousting, and riding; the evenings in singing to the harpsichord or the lute, or in parlor games, and especially, under the guidance of the gentle Duchess and her brilliant sister-in-law, Emilia Pia, in long philosophic debates: Was it indeed true that matter was masculine and form feminine? What were the qualities required of the perfect courtier? And of the ideal woman? And what was the true nature of love? "It is," said Bembo, "nought but a desire to enjoy beauty, and since one can only desire what one knows, so knowledge must precede desire." But the highest love, he maintained, the Platonic, "is an emanation of the divine goodness . . . shining over all created things, like the sun's light." So, night after night, they talked, until the candles burned low and the ladies, in their stiff brocades and high, heavy headdresses, dispersed to bed, and the Duke went down to his great library, where the portrait of his father's old schoolmaster—placed beside the greatest classical philosophers and the Fathers of the Church—bore witness to the influence he had exerted, and to his pupil's gratitude: "Federigo to Vittorino da Feltre, his revered master, who by word and example instructed him in all human excellence."

Iris Origo's books include biographies of the poet Leopardi and of Byron's daughter Allegra; The Last Attachment, *about Byron's affair with Teresa Guiccioli; and* The Merchant of Prato, *a vivid reconstruction of fourteenth-century Italy.*

THE URBINO DIPTYCH

Piero della Francesca

A major patron of the arts whose tastes had been shaped in Vittorino da Feltre's school, Federigo da Montefeltro is himself the subject of one of the most arresting portraits of the Renaissance (opposite). This is one half of the famous diptych painted by Piero della Francesca; the other is a portrait of Federigo's wife, Battista Sforza (page 72). They are paired so that husband and wife face each other, Federigo on the right and Battista on the left.

Commanding, virile, grave, Duke Federigo of Urbino is set like a monument against the idealized landscape. His extraordinary profile is the result of a jousting accident in which he lost an eye and had his nose broken.

Battista's portrait, like her personality, is in a fainter tone. She appears to have had a most thorough education as a little Humanist aristocrat (at the age of four she delivered a Latin oration in public), and possessed, besides, a natural sedateness and wisdom that enabled her to act as her husband's regent during his absences in time of war. She was his second wife, married when she was only fourteen; and she presented him with six daughters (one of them, Agnesina, became the mother of the famous Vittoria Colonna). She died giving birth to her only son, Guidobaldo.

On the reverse of each of the portraits is an allegorical "Triumph." Federigo's (page 70) shows him being crowned by Fame on his chariot and attended by the four Cardinal Virtues: Justice, Prudence, Fortitude, and Temperance. The Latin inscription, in Sapphic meter, reads, "Peer of the greatest leaders, he is borne in regal triumph, holding the sceptre nobly and glorified by the undying fame of his virtues." Battista (page 71) is drawn in her chariot by unicorns, which symbolize purity as well as death, and she is attended by the Theological Virtues: Faith, Hope, and Charity. Her inscription reads, "Even as it was with her in her great days, so she still lives on the lips of all men, adorned by the glory of her illustrious husband's deeds."

The precise date of these portraits is not certain. Most critics think it was about 1465, but Lionello Venturi dates them 1472, the year Battista died (he points out that the inscription below her Triumph is in the past tense, and that her face resembles a waxen death mask). Piero's diptych is now one of the glories of the Uffizi Gallery in Florence.

CLARVS INSIGNI VEHITVR TRIVMPHO ·
QVEM PAREM SVMMIS DVCIBVS PERHENNIS ·
FAMA VIRTVTVM CELEBRAT DECENTER ·
SCEPTRA TENENTEM

QVE MODVM REBVS TENVIT SECVNDIS ·
CONIVGIS MAGNI DECORATA RERVM ·
LAVDE GESTARVM VOLITAT PER ORA ·
CVNCTA VIRORVM ⟲

A MIRROR OF RENAISSANCE MAN

It was through Petrarch, as much as any one man, that Italy moved from the medieval world onto the threshold of the Renaissance. He was quite aware of this, and in 1352 commented wryly on his role in the revival of learning:

Is it then true that this disease of writing, like other malignant disorders, is, as the Satirist claims, incurable, and, as I begin to fear, contagious as well? How many, do you reckon, have caught it from me? Within our memory, it was rare enough for people to write verses. But now there is no one who does not write them; few indeed write anything else. . . . Even carpenters, fullers, and ploughmen leave the implements of their calling to talk of Apollo and the Muses. I cannot say how far the plague, which lately was confined to a few, has now spread.

From *Petrarch, the First Modern Scholar and Man of Letters,* J. H. Robinson and H. W. Rolfe, Putnam 1898

Leon Battista Alberti, who was called to Mantua to design the basilica of Sant' Andrea for Ludovico Gonzaga, left behind him a famous portrait of the educated "universal man." It may be somewhat disconcerting to discover that the man he was actually describing was Leon Battista Alberti (himself). But false modesty was not among the Renaissance ideals, of which this remains an accurate catalogue:

His genius was so versatile that you might almost judge all the fine arts to be his. . . . He played ball, hurled the javelin, ran, leaped, wrestled, and above all delighted in the steep ascent of mountains. . . . As a youth he excelled in warlike games. With his feet together, he could leap over the shoulders of men standing by. . . . With his left foot lifted from the ground to the wall of a church, he could throw an apple into the air so high that it would go far beyond the top of the highest roofs. . . . Strange and marvellous! that the most spirited horses and those most impatient of riders would, when he first mounted them, tremble violently and shudder as if in great fear. He learned music without teachers, and his compositions were approved by learned musicians. . . . But in truth, because he could not live without letters, at the age of twenty-four he turned to physics and the mathematical arts. . . . When he heard that a learned man of any kind had arrived, he would at once work his way into a position of familiarity with him and thus from any source whatsoever he began to learn what he was ignorant of. . . . When

his favourite dog died he wrote a funeral oration for him.

Whatever was done by man with genius and with a certain grace, he held to be almost divine; and he so respected anything achieved that he insisted even poor writers were worthy of praise. The sight of gems, flowers, and especially pleasant places more than once restored him from illness to good health.

From *The Viking Portable Renaissance Reader,* translated by James Bruce Ross

Vittorino's pupil, Federigo da Montefeltro, seemed even to his contemporaries the ideal man of the age. So he appears to the Humanist scholar Marsilio Ficino, writing in 1492 to Paul of Middelburg:

For this century, like a golden age, has restored to light the liberal arts, which were almost extinct: grammar, poetry, rhetoric, painting, sculpture, architecture, music, the ancient singing of songs to the Orphic lyre, and all this in Florence. Achieving what had been honored among the ancients, but almost forgotten since, the age has joined wisdom with eloquence, and prudence with the military art, and this most strikingly in Federigo, Duke of Urbino, as if proclaimed in the presence of Pallas herself, and it has made his son and his brother the heirs of his virtue.

From *The Viking Portable Renaissance Reader,* translated by Mary Martin McLaughlin

The perfect handbook of Renaissance conduct was eventually written by Baldassare Castiglione. In describing the polished manners and intellectual ardor that characterized the court of Guidobaldo da Montefeltro at Urbino, he projected an image of the ideal courtier:

I would have him more than passably learned in letters, at least in those studies which we call the humanities. Let him be conversant not only with the Latin language, but with Greek as well, because of the abundance and variety of things that are so divinely written therein. Let him be versed in the poets, as well as in the orators and historians, and let him be practiced also in writing verse and prose, especially in our own vernacular; for, besides the personal satisfaction he will take in this, in this way he will never want for pleasant entertainment with the ladies, who are usually fond of such things.

From *The Book of the Courtier,* translated by Charles S. Singleton, Doubleday Anchor Books

A measure of the magnificence with which the concert grand piano is played by young American artists was established in 1958 in Moscow by a Texan. By sending torrents of Rachmaninoff and Tchaikovsky chords cascading over his audiences ever since that triumph, twenty-five-year-old Van Cliburn has become a sizable folk hero at home and a Peace-Through-Piano-Playing symbol around the world. Some of his vast celebrity has spilled over upon the dozen or more gifted young performers in the United States who are his equals in all the techniques of the pianists' craft but whose attitudes toward the art vary significantly from Cliburn's.

They range from twenty-seven-year-old Glenn Gould, a young intellectual who plays Bach and his predecessors and Schoenberg and his followers but little in between, to twenty-six-year-old John Browning, a marvel of technique who formerly orbited in as romantic a realm as does Cliburn but currently shows signs of being drawn from it. Between these extremes are Seymour Lipkin, a reluctant pianist turned aspiring conductor, and a trio of performers in their early thirties whose musicianship is as solid as a C major triad: Eugene Istomin, Gary Graffman, and Leon Fleisher; together they constitute a central triumvirate among the Young American Pianists.

To Cliburn's six companions in this survey, the concert grand piano is an instrument of musical expression played from the floor up by the feet, the hands, and the head. Most of what the feet must do is determined by the hands, and what the hands must do has been completely prescribed by the composer. The role of the head, which these musicians take to be of towering importance, is never explicitly indicated in the notation but is always resolutely implied. They favor music of intellectual substance over inventions devised to aid pianists in performing acrobatics—a preference which leads them to much Beethoven and very little Liszt. And in those stretches of the piano literature where emotion can easily slop over, they turn cool or even ice-cold and play almost metronomic Chopin.

Living by these precepts, though at times observing them imperfectly, the Young American Pianists represent a reform movement operating against the excesses of the Grand Mannered Romantic Virtuosos Club. The Club, a nineteenth-century institution, had Franz Liszt as both its founder and perhaps finest representative. *"Le concert, c'est moi!"* he proclaimed regularly, and he always meant it. His appearances constituted musical soliloquies, with the flamboyant Hungarian doing almost all the playwriting for his own act. A program he gave in Rome in 1839 consisted of (1) the overture to *William Tell* as transcribed by Liszt, (2) themes from *I Puritani* woven into a fantasy by Liszt, (3) an array of Liszt's own compositions played by the composer, and (4) an improvisation on one of the composer's own themes played by Franz Liszt. In his book *Men, Women and Pianos,* Arthur Loesser cites a Vienna critic's account of the Hungarian's platform manner: "Liszt . . . is an amiable fiend who treats his mistress—the piano—now tenderly, now tyrannically, devours her with kisses, lacerates her with lustful bites, embraces her, caresses her, sulks with her, scolds her, rebukes her, grabs her by the hair, clasps her then all the more delicately, more affectionately, more passionately, more flamingly, more meltingly; exults with her to the heavens, soars with her through all the skies and finally settles down with her in a vale of flowers covered with a canopy of stars."

TEXT CONTINUED ON PAGE 81

Almost to a man, these rising young Americans lean away from virtuoso tradition and toward cerebral playing of classics. The exception: Van Cliburn

SEVEN KEYBOARD INSURGENTS

By JOSEPH RODDY

GLENN GOULD sighs and writhes during performances and seems to be as deep in artistic torment as an old-style romantic virtuoso while he plays the eighteenth-century classics and the twelve-tone modern repertoire with equally severe, impersonal precision. "I can hardly bear to look at him during a recital," says another young pianist, "but I'll go through even that misery to hear him." The twenty-seven-year-old master musician from Toronto was first acclaimed in the United States for his recording of the Bach Goldberg Variations. His later recordings of Alban Berg and Ernst Krenek sonatas have been hailed as enthusiastically in the United States as his Beethoven concerto performances were in Moscow a year before Van Cliburn's triumph there. A graduate at twelve of the Toronto Conservatory, Gould has become a part-time composer (a string quartet finished, an opera started) and a full-time eccentric, carrying about his own supply of bottled spring water and electric heaters against the cold of the concert halls.

GARY GRAFFMAN (left) has won most of the competitions which young American pianists can enter—the Leventritt and the Rachmaninoff contests among them—and since his child prodigy days has steadily continued to enlarge his artistry. A sharply percussive attack upon the instrument was once an identifiable Graffman trait. But in his recent recording of the Brahms D minor Concerto with the Boston Symphony Orchestra, he has knit together the lines of the slow movement with a sense of lyric style worthy of Artur Rubinstein, whom Graffman regards as one of the greatest living pianists. The thirty-one-year-old Graffman studied with Isabelle Vengerova of the Curtis Institute of Music in Philadelphia and has been counseled by both Vladimir Horowitz and Rudolf Serkin. A performer at the piano since the age of four, Graffman today possesses a vast repertoire, and he is as strong in the eighteenth-century classics as in the nineteenth-century romantics and the twentieth-century schools of piano literature. He has appeared with orchestras around the world, from the great capitals of Europe to remote Australian towns.

EUGENE ISTOMIN (opposite), in the opinion of Graffman and Leon Fleisher, two of his closest pianist friends, is entitled to eminence in their confraternity because he was once water boy for the Brooklyn Dodgers. Istomin's teacher was Rudolf Serkin, but the thirty-four-year-old pianist is quick to point out that he has been heavily influenced also by the ideas of Toscanini and the violin of Heifetz. Istomin holds that no one today plays any instrument as well as Heifetz plays his. Hence, at one stage in his student days, Istomin regularly clamped his thumbs under the keyboard while his fingers applied a violinist's vibrato to the piano keys. Istomin imagined that this colored and sustained sound, but his friends assured him that it did not. Today his intellectual grasp of music and easy air of self-assurance have put him in the position of being sought out as an arbiter by even younger pianists. Istomin has recorded Bach, Beethoven, Mozart, Schubert, Handel, and Rachmaninoff works. "No ten minutes of my waking life have gone by in which I did not think about music," he says. "The only thing I tire of is practicing."

LEON FLEISHER (left) established a sizable reputation in 1952 when he won the important Queen Elisabeth International Music Competition in Belgium. There, among other feats of musical strength, he had to learn in one week a concerto he had never seen or heard before. Afterwards he swept through the Brahms D minor Concerto with a splendor that so impressed the judges that Fleisher has since become virtually the Belgian court musician. Even the Queen—the world's only fiddling monarch—has at times joined him and Beryl Senofsky in Vivaldi sonatas for two violins. In the United States, when he was only ten, Fleisher began studying with Artur Schnabel, and as soon as he started associating with other young pianists, he learned that all of them envied his closeness to the late German master. Now thirty-one years old, Fleisher dates his independence as a performing artist from the day, not too long ago, when he listened again to one of the Beethoven sonatas recorded by Schnabel and decided that, although it was a beautiful performance, it was not precisely the performance he himself would give the next time he played it.

PHOTOGRAPHED FOR HORIZON BY EUGENE COOK

Seymour Lipkin (left) is a deeply reflective artist for whom the piano seems almost insufficient as an instrument of expression, and he shows inclinations to break away from it. Though magnificently skilled in the pianist's craft, Lipkin prefers to accept conducting assignments every time he has a chance (he has appeared in that role with the New York City Opera Company and the New York Philharmonic Symphony Orchestra). Like Graffman, Lipkin is a pianist who has mastered both the classical and romantic repertoires but has been heard at his best in the moderns—in Prokofiev, in Stravinsky, and in Leonard Bernstein's *Age of Anxiety* (a symphony with a concerto-sized piano part tailored to accommodate its composer, another reluctant pianist). Rudolf Serkin was his teacher, and Lipkin himself has taught regularly at the Berkshire Music Festival at Tanglewood, where his subject is conducting. At his New York studio he teaches piano to advanced students who seem likely to abide with the instrument. Of the young pianists of first rank, Lipkin is one of the smallest money-makers on the recital circuits. But on the scale of artistic value established by Artur Schnabel, on which serious musicianship is of a higher order than instrumental skill, Lipkin is pre-eminently successful.

John Browning (below) first studied piano with his mother, passed through a succession of teachers, and came into the care of Mme Rosina Lhevinne. He won the Leventritt Award, made a New York debut with the New York Philharmonic but, although proceeding respectably, caused little stir until Van Cliburn emerged into world fame through his own Russian triumph. That sensation led to a certain amount of groping to recognize young American pianists at home before the Russians found them. The first beneficiary of this search was Browning, a twenty-six-year-old musician from the American West and a Juilliard schoolmate of Cliburn's who had been runner-up to the Russian Vladimir Ashkenazy at the Brussels Competition in 1956 where, under the approving eye of his friend Leon Fleisher, he played the Brahms B flat major Concerto with notable effect. Though his manner is too mature and restrained to attain full virtuoso effect, Browning has mastered all the acknowledged showpieces. He plays them less frequently each year. He is now a pianist in transition, somewhat favoring the cerebral over the romantic repertoires, and he is moving with equal facility through the keyboard compositions of Mozart, Beethoven, and Schubert, as well as Chopin, Debussy, and Ravel.

That is the way Liszt treated the art of the piano, and the preposterousness of it was pointed out by the perceptive Clara Schumann, wife of Robert Schumann, who observed that before Liszt, pianists played, and after him they pounded or whispered. "He has the decline of piano playing on his conscience," she remarked. After Liszt's recital career ended, virtuosoism continued to thrive in such showmen as Sigismond Thalberg and then sloped off early in this century with Ignace Jan Paderewski. Today it survives only vestigially with Artur Rubinstein, or possibly young Van Cliburn himself. What the virtuosos had in common was a preference for programs that favored the tinseled and easy-appeal stretches of the repertoire, because what they played mattered less than the personal manner in which they played it. Since Clara Schumann herself, the restorative influences of such serious artists as Ferruccio Busoni, Alfred Cortot, Edwin Fischer, and most importantly, Artur Schnabel and Rudolf Serkin in our own time have brought about a major shift in the public's taste and in pianists' programs and performing styles. We are witnessing a revival of interest in the severely written piano music of those earlier composers who are often termed classical. The gaudy nineteenth-century showpieces, for the most part, have now passed out of style, and the Young American Pianists—with an exception to be made chiefly for Van Cliburn, himself a latter-day romantic—are at the peak of a trend toward cerebration at the keyboard.

There would be cause for show of patriotic puffing-up about this new national musical resource if it could be established that the young pianists were all inside-and-out American-made products, in the way that basketball players and rock-'n'-roll idols are. But of the seven young pianists considered here, Glenn Gould is a Canadian, although his reputation, for the most part, was made in the United States. All the others were born here, but none of their principal teachers were. Three of them (Cliburn, Browning, and Fleisher) became celebrated at home only after being lionized abroad. And only two in the group (Gould and Cliburn) yet have enough box-office pulling power to fill Carnegie Hall for a recital. When they play there, a fair segment of the audience is made up of piano teachers, on hand to determine for themselves whether "cool"—intellectual—piano playing of the style of Gould's is here to stay or whether Grand Virtuosoism is due for a comeback.

Until recently, the dominant influences in piano teaching in America were Mmes. Rosina Lhevinne, of the Juilliard School of Music in New York, and the late Isabelle Vengerova, of the Curtis Institute of Music in Philadelphia, both of them formidable Russians with a lingering reverence for the accomplishments of the Grand Mannered Virtuosos. Mme Lhevinne was the teacher of Cliburn and Browning; Mme Vengerova of Graffman. In recent years the attitudes and techniques taught by the late Artur Schnabel and the now brilliantly active Rudolf Serkin have largely replaced those of the two ladies among young pianists here. Schnabel, born in Austria, was less concerned with digital agility than with the mastery over the substance of music that comes from studying its structure and relating its phrases to one another, like a grammarian parsing and reassembling a sentence. Schnabel's heavily annotated edition of the thirty-two Beethoven sonatas, along with his recorded performances of the entire set, have become a *summa musica* that serious young piano students pore over and listen to constantly. Since Schnabel's death in 1951, the Bohemian-born Serkin has carried on most of his precepts. Aspiring pianists from all over the United States have closed in on Serkin or come under his artistic influence. Among his students were Seymour Lipkin and Eugene Istomin.

In the measurable specifics of piano playing, all of the pianists grouped here are fairly matched technical wizards who can toss off tortuous passages with every appearance of ease. They are all keenly interested in other aspects of their art, from modern opera to *musique concrète*. Each of them is articulate about the frustrating reality that a piano is an instrument incapable of sustaining tone the way string and and reed instruments do. For this, and other reasons, none of them regards the piano as the solar center of the musical universe—a quality signifying an openness of spirit rarely encountered among performing artists. Unlike practically all other instrumentalists, singers, and conductors, they are banded together into something dangerously close to a mutual admiration society. When together, they may agree on a few points about music, but may as readily fall into a dispute over the public relations aspects of their profession. To a man, for all their closeness, they deplore being labeled as the Young American Pianists, because the prospect of announcing one day that they are now the Middle-Aged American Pianists and then the Old American Pianists depresses them.

Joseph Roddy, who has also written the captions accompanying this article, is an editor of Life. *His commentary on music has also appeared in the* Encyclopædia Britannica.

V AN CLIBURN, the gangling pianist who musically is this century's closest facsimile of Franz Liszt, stands almost alone as a countertrend to the inclinations of most young American pianists. The huge-handed Texan plays the big romantic pieces in a big romantic way, and the astonishing sales figures run up by his recordings of concertos that overpowered the Soviets are causing his contemporaries in the United States to wonder at times whether they have taken too large a lead on the tastes of their audiences. Cliburn's own problem is of another order. It is whether the demands made on him as a symbol of American superiority will ever let up, so that he can concentrate on practicing at the piano. When he played a Mozart concerto with the New York Philharmonic last season, critics felt that he seemed beyond his depth. And in London, some months later, he was sharply rebuked for his performance of Beethoven. As a musical stunt man—with an act that the public will not necessarily ever tire of—Cliburn possibly could sustain the hero status he achieved in Moscow without enriching his musicianship. But he is far too sensitive a young man to settle for that.

By J. CHRISTOPHER HEROLD

The Pleasures of the Bastille

Servants, fine cuisine, and courteous jailers were the due of the King's incarcerated "guests." There was leisure for music, literature, and love. But one lack of this model prison was that its inmates did not know when, if ever, they would be freed

Historians of all political shades will readily concede that the storming of the Bastille of Paris, on July 14, 1789, was not in itself a glorious action. It was instigated by shady men for shady motives, carried out by a disreputable mob, and abetted by disloyal soldiers. The defenders—a handful of invalid veterans and their officers—capitulated almost without resistance. Despite the terms of capitulation, the mob killed the commandant and two of his officers; a scullion boy, skilled in the art of meat cutting, severed the commandant's head, which was then paraded about on the point of a pike. The total number of prisoners liberated from the huge fortress was seven. Of these, four had been detained for forgery and disappeared immediately. A fifth, a young debauchee held on his family's request, allowed himself to be feted by the revolutionary societies and made

Henri Masers de Latude and a fellow prisoner engineered the Bastille's most famous escape—a feat commemorated in this portrait of him by Antoine Vestier. Latude was recaptured in Amsterdam and locked up for another twenty-eight years, during which he wrote his Memoirs. *Published after his release in 1784, they were an immediate success, went through many editions, and grew more improbable with each.*

speeches announcing the dawn of freedom. The other two, who were madmen, were carried through the streets on the shoulders of their liberators and then hastily locked up in the insane asylum of Charenton.

These facts are well known, and there is no intention, in repeating them here, of "debunking" an action that is commemorated every year as a national holiday in France. Inglorious and unnecessary though it was, the storming of the Bastille is traditionally regarded as the beginning of the French Revolution; the dignity and significance it lacked were conferred on the deed by the generous hopes it stirred, by the tremendous events it set in motion, and by the symbolic significance that attached to the Bastille itself.

Very soon after its capture, one hundred and seventy years ago, the Bastille was razed. Its destruction was intended to symbolize the destruction of feudalism and tyranny. Yet it would be difficult to name another building of which not a stone has been left for nearly two centuries whose image yet remains as vividly and accurately present to the popular mind. Its outward aspect has been preserved by innumerable prints, reproduced in textbooks, histories, and dictionaries. Its huge, forbidding walls and towers, its outer walls and moats and drawbridge remain engraved in the imagination of

This drawing of the Bastille as it appeared in 1789 is signed (upper right) by Pierre François Palloy, who took charge of demolishing it after its seizure. He used eight hundred men to tear it down, and sold off the locks, keys, and leg irons as souvenirs.

posterity with all the sharpness of the engravings that preserved them. This massive, arrogant anachronism, towering above the nondescript houses of the surrounding districts, seems indeed a permanent act of provocation. What is more, it conjures up an image of grim, dank cells and dungeons, where pale, white-haired, and—needless to say—innocent prisoners, clothed in rags and rattling chains, were kept on bread and water until they died—usually mad.

The truth is that life in the Bastille bore a closer resemblance to comic opera than to Grand-Guignol. It is not suggested that to be an inmate of the Bastille was particularly desirable (though, as will be seen, some inmates found it so), or that the system of arbitrary detention without trial merits defense. But never before or since in history was there a prison quite like the Bastille in the eighteenth century.

The grim exterior of the Bastille and the lurid legends about what went on inside symbolize, though they immensely exaggerate, a certain truth: the fortress *was* an anachronistic survival of the feudal age, and its inmates, though for the most part by no means innocent, were detained arbitrarily and without trial. Yet if there is anything that symbolizes the last years of the *ancien régime*, it is not the medieval façade of the Bastille and the fanciful legends about it, but the bizarre and benign system that prevailed inside it. A prison system often reflects certain features of the society outside. Like the *ancien régime* as a whole, the regime of the Bastille was a patchwork of special and contradictory rules and traditions, an agglomeration of exceptional cases. Individuals were

84

not treated according to an easily ascertainable set of rules of law or equity. Each was treated according to his own status, his means, his connections, and his ability to use his wits. Injustice was administered with a maximum of politeness and humane concern for its victims by jailers of exquisitely refined sensibility. And the humaneness with which the prisoners were treated was jealously hidden from the outside world by a senseless security system which cherished secrecy and mystery for their own sakes.

The Bastille never was a prison in the proper sense of the word. It was a military fortress. Its cornerstone was laid about 1370, but it began to be used as a prison only under Cardinal Richelieu. By the beginning of the eighteenth century it had lost all military significance; its garrison consisted of invalid soldiers, and its sole function became that of a state prison. Yet although its inmates were placed under the authority of the Lieutenant General of Police, the fortress itself remained in theory a military establishment, and the prisoners were guests of the King.

The word "guests" is used advisedly here. The inmates of the Bastille were, with some exceptions, "state prisoners": persons who might, in one sense or another, be considered dangerous to the security of the state if they were left free, but whom the state did not wish to put to trial. (The exceptions were, for the most part, transients who eventually were transferred to other institutions.) To imprison or release a person all that was needed was a royal order, or *lettre de cachet,* countersigned by a minister. The order could originate either with the government or with any private person with the right connections. Its purpose was simply to put an inconvenient person out of the way for a convenient length of time, without the formality of a trial. Indeed there often was no basis for a trial, and even if there was a clear basis, it was deemed undesirable to hold one. A trial might have bared matters which either the government or the prisoner or his family preferred to hush up. Sometimes the reasons for detention were purely preventive or pedagogical; thus a father might have his son locked up to prevent him from fighting a duel, or to induce him to meditate for a few months.

Of course, there were unfortunate cases of men held for many years without anyone's knowing why, and it was at any rate disquieting not to know whether one's imprisonment would last a week, a year, or a lifetime. But nearly everyone in the Bastille had a duke or a minister among his acquaintance, or perhaps the duke's or minister's mistress, or at least his valet or cook: the same system of personal influence which allowed private persons to secure an order of arrest eventually also enabled them to secure an order of release. Most prisoners, had they been bound over for trial, would have suffered a harsher and longer imprisonment, if not worse. And there was an additional advantage in not undergoing trial. Since torture was part of the judicial process, and since by the seventeenth century there was no judicial process at

the Bastille, there also was no torture. Justice and medicine had this in common—that usually a man was better off without the benefit of either.

All the prisoners were the King's guests. Some were paying guests; the others, who could not pay for their upkeep, were his pensioners. The majority were suspected spies or political plotters, indiscreet pamphleteers, religious dissenters (especially Jansenists and Protestants), blackmailers, poisoners, and sorcerers with exalted clienteles, insubordinate or duel-loving officers, indiscreet lovers, counterfeiters, forgers, lunatics with a bent for politics, ladies who ran gambling dens, immoral priests, men of letters who had exercised their wit on the wrong people, spendthrift sons of noble houses, and debauchees. A few, to be sure, were truly innocent victims. To that last category belonged the most famous of the prisoners of the Bastille, the Man with the Iron Mask, whose mask was made of black velvet, whose death certificate bears the name Marchioly, and about whose identity historians and romancers wrote endlessly until it was established with reasonable certainty that his name was indeed Marchioly—or, more accurately, Mattioli. As the secretary of state to the Duke of Mantua, he had double-crossed a scheme of Louis XIV and was kidnapped across the border by the French. Understandably, Louis XIV did not wish to advertise the incident; and he took such elaborate precautions to hide his prisoner's identity that when the prisoner died, not even the authorities of the Bastille could remember who he was, why he was there, or why he had to wear a mask.

The roster of the Bastille's inmates contains such exalted names as the Duc de Richelieu, Voltaire, the Cardinal de Rohan, and the Marquis de Mirabeau. Equally typical, however, were such men as the Abbé Fleur, an ecclesiastic who, at the time of his arrest for forging royal lottery tickets, was domiciled in a bordello; a confidence man named Dubuisson, who had negotiated a loan of 15,000,000 livres from the devil to the Duc d'Olonne, with the soul of the Duc as collateral; the Marquis de Sade; and the Abbé de Moncrif, dean of the Cathedral of Autun, who had debauched two girls, his wards, and got one of them with child, besides being in debt for 70,000 livres, being a party in seventeen simultaneous lawsuits, and having stirred up, while under arrest in an ecclesiastic jail, a rebellion among his fellow inmates and driven his superiors out of their wits by raising chickens and ducks in his quarters.

As a rule, a person against whom a *lettre de cachet* had been issued was arrested by a police officer. There were cases, however, especially in earlier days, when the order to surrender at the Bastille was transmitted directly to the person to be detained. Thus there is the account of the young noble under Louis XIV who received his *lettre de cachet* in the morning, went hunting with the King, and then excused himself to the King, explaining that he had received the King's orders to be at the Bastille at such and such a time.

Services Culturels Français

The legendary "Man in the Iron Mask" was real, but his mask was black velvet and his "crime" a political double cross.

The King graciously gave him permission to leave the hunt.

In the less feudal eighteenth century, the prisoner would be taken to the fortress in a hired cab, with curtains drawn. The cab would stop at the drawbridge and be challenged by the sergeant of the guard. The arresting officer would reply, "Order of the King!" whereupon the sergeant and the other soldiers on sentry duty would execute an about-face, turning their backs on the cab. A bell was rung, the drawbridge lowered, and the cab proceeded to the inner court. The prisoner was then escorted to a large room, called the council chamber, where the governor of the fortress would receive him, sign the *lettre de cachet*, and, after a routine search, have the prisoner conducted to his room.

The guard would politely escort the prisoner to his new quarters, situated in one of the eight large towers of the fortress. The rooms were spacious, with high ceilings and large —though heavily barred—windows and a fireplace. The furniture was austere but adequate. If the prisoner had the means, he could have his own furniture brought in. One abbé's furniture included five armchairs, eight straight chairs, a desk, a small table, three paintings, and two wall tapestries. Some prisoners had harpsichords and other musical instruments. The writer La Beaumelle brought a library of six hundred volumes. The Marquis de Sade, who wrote a large part of his novels in the Bastille, had his walls covered from end to end with crimson hangings. Prisoners of particularly high rank sometimes were given entire apartments and moved in with a suite of retainers as well as their furniture.

As for food at the Bastille, it was quite adequate. The King's allowance for meals varied from three livres a day for the lowest class of prisoner to thirty-six livres for a marshal of France. A typical three-livre-a-day dinner consisted of *soupe aux croûtes,* beef, sheep's tongue *en ragoût,* and dessert. A ten-livre fare on meatless days might offer crayfish bisque and six courses of fish. One prisoner, who declared that he could not eat butcher's meat, was fed on fowl and venison exclusively. Another, describing the rigor of the Bastille in a pamphlet written after his release, cited the following menu:

Green pea soup, garnished with lettuce and a joint of fowl

Sliced roast beef, garnished with parsley

Meat pie, garnished with sweetbreads, coxcombs, asparagus, mushrooms, and truffles

Sheep's tongue en ragoût

Biscuit, Fruit, Burgundy wine

Distinguished prisoners often were invited to the governor's table. The writer and later revolutionist Linguet accused the authorities of the Bastille of trying to overfeed him in order to poison him. If this was so, the authorities were unsuccessful: Linguet lived on for many years, and the authority that killed him in 1792 was the guillotine.

There is only one recorded instance of a prisoner complaining about his food. On a Friday in October, 1753, at eight in the evening, a prisoner named Danry, alias Latude, who at the time was kept in solitary confinement, could be heard roaring even louder than was his wont. When the jailer hurried to his cell, Danry asked to see the Major (the executive officer) of the Bastille without delay. The Major arrived; Danry declared in a thunderous voice that he ate neither eggs nor artichokes nor spinach, and requested that a man be dispatched immediately to the Halles to buy him fish. The Major pointed out that this was hardly the time for shopping. Flying into another paroxysm of rage, Danry declared that he was short of shirts and linen. The Major pointed out that Danry owned seven shirts, four of them brand-new; Danry responded only with a new fit. Soon afterward, by order of the Lieutenant General of the Police, Danry received, at the King's expense, two dozen shirts at ten dollars apiece and a supply of cambric handkerchiefs.

Danry's passion for shirts and linen seems extraordinary. In his memoirs he declares that at one point during his long imprisonment he owned 162 shirts, twelve dozen pairs of silk stockings, eighteen pairs of socks, and three dozen napkins, all furnished free by the government.

If food and clothing were abundant, drink was no less so for those who desired it. One of the two madmen liberated on July 14, 1789, had consumed in the space of three months twelve bottles of brandy, 121 bottles of beer, and 167 bottles of wine. Indeed, since the prisoners were held in the Bastille as a measure of precaution rather than punishment, the authorities made life as easy for them as they could. Those who could afford it, to be sure, were expected to pay for their food, furnishings, clothing, and servants, but to those who had no money the King gave an ample pension. What they did not spend on their needs, they could keep. Under King Louis XIV this pension was paid directly to the prisoners; later on the system was modified, and the money was paid to the administrators of the Bastille. Still, the prisoners were entitled to an accounting, and if an unspent balance remained at the time of their release, it was paid to them. There are instances of prisoners requesting to stay on in order to increase their nest egg. Many of the prisoners, upon leaving, were indemnified or even granted pensions (as was Voltaire, for instance).

One of the most peculiar features of life at the Bastille was the rule governing personal servants. Prisoners could bring in servants either at their own expense or, by special permission (notably in cases of long confinement), at the King's expense. For a servant's wages the government was willing to spend nine hundred livres a year. But even more peculiar was the provision that if a servant agreed to take employment in the Bastille, he also had to agree to remain there until his master was liberated.

Locked up in 1719, justifiably, for plotting against the Regent, the Duc de Richelieu enjoyed the frequent visits of his two mistresses —one of whom was the Regent's daughter.

Like everything else in the Bastille, prison discipline varied considerably from case to case. As a rule, prisoners were interrogated by the Lieutenant General of the Police within twenty-four hours of their arrival. Interrogation might continue sporadically for days, weeks, or months, and until it was completed a prisoner was held strictly incommunicado. There is every indication that normally the prisoners were questioned politely, without any use or threat of force, though with a great deal of paternal admonition. When this stage was completed, the prisoner might be granted various privileges. If he wished, he might be allowed to share his room with another prisoner, visit with other prisoners, take walks on the platforms of the towers, receive visitors from outside, or leave his room at will in order to walk or play in the courtyard—a privilege called the *liberté de la cour*. To grant or withdraw such privileges, the Governor of the Bastille had to receive special authorization from the Lieutenant General of the Police.

Needless to say, the primary considerations in the granting of special privileges were the rank of the prisoner and the degree of secrecy with which he was to be surrounded. The first of these criteria was fairly clear-cut; all other things being equal, a duke enjoyed more comfort than a barber's apprentice. The security criterion, however, was often of a rather nebulous nature. The Lieutenant General of the Police did not always inform the Governor of the Bastille why a ward of his was regarded as a threat to the state, and sometimes the Lieutenant General of the Police himself did not know.

It is clear from many of the published documents that these authorities often tried to obtain the release of a prisoner, or at least a liberalizing of his treatment, and were repeatedly frustrated in their attempts by an unexplained "No" from Versailles.

The more fashionable inmates of the Bastille enjoyed, for the most part, a rather active social life. They gave parties for each other and for outside visitors; some of these entertainments were as brilliant and lavish as any given in the more conventional salons of Paris. Mademoiselle de Launay, lady-in-waiting to the Duchesse de Maine, who spent the years 1718–20 in the Bastille for her part in a plot against the Regent, recalled that period as the happiest in her life.

This statement is more easily understood if one knows that the only time Mademoiselle de Launay knew love was during her imprisonment. She acquired two lovers: one, an officer of the Bastille, who acted like a perfect gentleman but with whom she was not in love; the other, a fellow inmate and fellow conspirator, with whom she fell passionately in love but who did not act quite like a gentleman. In one of the more bizarre episodes related in her memoirs, she tells how, one evening, the turnkey unwittingly locked her *amant du coeur* into her room, and how her jailer-lover, to whom she frantically signaled from her window, obligingly let her prisoner-lover out and never breathed a word.

For relaxation, those prisoners who were not restricted to their rooms could go bowling in the courtyard or take other exercise. In 1788 twelve Breton noblemen requested a billiard table and obtained it. Others raised dogs, birds, and many generations of cats (but not, contrary to legend, spiders). Many had musical instruments. The Duc de Richelieu and Mademoiselle de Launay, his neighbor, sang operatic duets from their windows and were joined by other inmates for ensembles and choruses. The prison library was well stocked. Under the regime of Lieutenant General of the Police Berryer, in the 1750's, such unusual concern was shown for the prisoners' morale that an order banned a religious poem from the library as being "too melancholy."

The prisoners' religious needs were not entirely ignored. The prison chapel contained several closetlike structures in which the inmates could attend Mass unseen by each other and by the priest. These closets were frequently used as mailboxes, and a lively clandestine correspondence took place among the prisoners.

Nearly everybody wrote. Pens, ink, and paper were liberally provided. One prisoner, it is true—Danry, the collector of linen and hosiery—chose instead to write to the authorities with his blood, on strips of linen or bread tablets, a habit which offended the sensibilities of the Lieutenant General of the Police. Yet whenever inquiry was made of the governor as to why the prisoner Danry was not supplied with writing materials, the reply was, invariably, that the materials had indeed been given the prisoner, but that he chose this unappetizing method of communication instead.

The nature of the prisoners' writings varied a great deal. In the Bastille Voltaire revised his *Oedipe* and wrote part of the *Henriade*; De Sade, amid his crimson hangings, wrote away at his novels; the writer La Beaumelle, who was addicted to hoaxing, wrote love letters, purportedly from a lady, to his fellow prisoner Allègre, a schoolteacher who wrote memoranda to the government on a variety of subjects including mathematics, engineering, and architecture; Allègre's roommate Danry, in turn, wrote memoranda on balancing the budget and on postal reform; and all, of course, wrote petitions. The prison authorities were no less literary; their reports to higher authorities testify that they had ample leisure to polish their literary style and adorn it with flowers of wit.

Men of letters, who were well represented in the Bastille, formed a special group in the sense that temporary imprisonment in that fortress represented an indispensable phase in their careers. "My career opened up before me," wrote the Abbé Morellet of his imprisonment. "Those six months in the Bastille were to be an excellent recommendation and an infallible road to success." When he was released, the Abbé exclaimed, "God bless those good tyrants!" Marmontel, whose reputation was at its peak when he was held in the Bastille, was treated as a guest of honor by the prison chiefs and left with equally benign feelings toward them. These experiences prevented neither Morellet nor Marmontel nor their friends among the *philosophes* from publicly inveighing against the cruel tyranny of their imprisonment; indeed, it was in their interest to contribute to the legend of the Bastille.

Not every prisoner, of course, was lionized by his jailers as Marmontel was, and life in the Bastille was by no means a bed of roses for lower-class persons caught in an infraction of the rules. There were punitive cells, some under the roofs and uncomfortably warm, some on the ground floor. The latter, *cachots,* were halfway underground, damp, and lit only by what daylight came in through a narrow loophole. Prisoners guilty of disciplinary infractions were often held there for months, in chains, and bedded on straw. They were not forgotten, however, and even to them the jailers extended whatever kindness they could under the regulations. Unfortunately, since many prisoners felt that they had been arrested without cause in the first place, they did not always appreciate the justice of being placed in disciplinary cells or always show gratitude for small favors. Thus the Major of the Bastille reported about Danry, who at the time was being held in a *cachot*, "Yesterday we had Danry taken out of his irons, and today he was given a cot, mattresses, a pillow, sheets, and a blanket, together with seeds for his birds, all this in accordance with your order of the first of the month. This prisoner, moreover, requested a different room, a new bed, a table, chairs, and a lamp or candle. I told him that he was pushing his pretensions beyond what was required of us."

Danry undoubtedly was not altogether sane, and many of the other long-term prisoners were plainly lunatics. Some became estranged from reality as a result of their long isolation, but for the most part their imprisonment merely brought into the open a psychotic predisposition which had landed them in the Bastille in the first place. In any event, they were better off than they would have been at Charenton, to which they were transferred only if they became violent. So accustomed were the jailers to the eccentricities of their wards that they did not recognize lunacy when they saw it. Thus the record of the prisoner Tavernier (a liquor-loving madman who was moved to Charenton in 1789) contains the following understatement: "His long imprisonment has given him an original character, so little in conformity with that of the people in the outside world that they would take him for a madman." Tavernier had spent thirty years in the Bastille at that time.

CONTINUED ON PAGE 128

By WALTER KERR

IN
SEARCH
OF
SHYLOCK

Sometimes played as a villain, sometimes as a tragic hero, Shakespeare's Venetian has long baffled actors and troubled sensitive audiences. What can be made of this great but equivocal role and of its author's intentions? A leading critic offers a solution to one of the theater's outstanding riddles

Shylock was portrayed as a comic character until the Irish actor Charles Macklin (near right) gave him a new guise—part Lear, part Simon Legree. This convention persisted through the nineteenth century in the work of such noted stars as W. C. Macready (far right).

Shakespeare is honored in many ways, but the most striking tribute we pay him today is in continuing to produce *The Merchant of Venice*.

Each production is, really, an act of faith, made in the face of the evidence. Every time anyone decides to mount the play he is saying, in effect, that Shakespeare cannot possibly have meant what he seems to mean, that the humane and penetrating intelligence we have come to know so well through thirty-six other plays could never have been capable of the unthinking, unfeeling anti-Semitism that poisons the portrait of Shylock.

The evidence to the contrary is formidable, both inside and outside the play. Within the fairy-tale structure of the piece, Shylock is most certainly the villain, a scoundrel whose harsh terms and ready knife constitute the only threat to the happiness of some of the nicest people who never lived. Shylock starves his servants, loves his ducats more than his daughter, and is altogether incapable of mercy. In addition to what Shakespeare has written there is the atmosphere in which he wrote: We know that the Jewish physician Lopez had just been executed for treason, that Marlowe's monstrous *Jew of Malta* had been making money in a rival playhouse, that the mood of the moment may very well have equated Jewishness with villainy. Shakespeare, great as he was, was also a man of his time: How can we be sure that *The Merchant of Venice* isn't an unconscious lapse on the part of a first-rate mind brought about by an error that was simply in the air, too much a commonplace to be questioned?

Stubbornly, and with a dogged intuition that there must

somewhere be an explanation that will confound the plot of the play and the facts of Elizabethan life, we keep plunging into the embarrassments of the work in the hope that, one time or another, an actor's or director's inspiration will penetrate the mystery at its heart. There are clues that actors and directors have made much of. The "Hath not a Jew eyes?" speech stands there, a sudden and puzzling invitation to sympathy. This hated Jew may yet be a man. Shylock, mourning the theft of his turquoise, pauses to remember that "I had it of Leah when I was a bachelor." This widower is clearly no monster. And, technically speaking, is Shylock ever wholly in the wrong? Antonio has understood and accepted the terms of the bond; no one has deceived him. Shylock never demands more than the terms of the bond; he is within his rights. The defeat of Shylock is not accomplished by strict justice, but by a trick. Isn't the Jew more sinned against than sinning?

The possibility that Shylock is as much a victim of Venetian society as certain improvident Venetians are the victims of his malice is the hint that has been most exhaustively explored in our time. The text has been all but X-rayed in the search for lines, phrases, hitherto unimagined attitudes that might help to justify Shylock and so acquit Shakespeare of the charge that is implicitly brought against him. In performance, all such lines, phrases, and attitudes have been carefully stressed; perhaps our commonest experience of the play in the theater is that of watching an edgy actor approach an uncomfortable passage with the thought, "How am I going to twist *this* scene so as to avoid offense and gain a little respect?" plainly written on his face. The other principals have been freshly re-examined. How admirable is this Antonio, who can barely refrain from spitting on a Jew while arrogantly taking his money? What sort of sponging fortune hunter is Bassanio, anyway? Can a more cold-blooded package than Jessica be imagined—a girl who abandons her father, steals his treasure, and turns Christian on demand?

From so much earnest inquiry has emerged a by now familiar Shylock: a man who is at the very least a dignified representative of an oppressed race and whose vigorous insistence upon his pound of flesh is the direct result of renewed insult, evasion, and betrayal by the Christian community; and a man who may, in the hands of a genuinely gifted actor, acquire something of the stature of a tragic hero, moving us to compassion and benediction as he stumbles brokenly from the courtroom.

Around him, the Venetian butterflies who pass their time in planning masked revels, marriages by guessing games, gay boy-girl disguises, and coy exchanges of rings, dance out their ephemeral lives under varying shades of light. In one production they become a tinseled, irresponsibly charming counterpoint to the main, more sober business of the evening. In another, they become a faintly melancholy echo of a romantic world that is vanishing under the burden of Venetian commerce and business-by-bond. In the production that may have brought every facet of our contemporary reinterpretation of the play into an ultimate balance—Tyrone Guthrie's staging for star Frederick Valk at Stratford, Ontario, in 1955 —the sporting bloods of the Rialto were, for the most part, decadent bigots; Antonio and Bassanio were latent homosexuals, Belmont was peopled with opportunists, and the entire company joined forces in hissing, hooting, and spitting a stricken woolly bear of a Shylock out of the play. If this last series of images seems in any way excessive, it must also be said that Mr. Guthrie has given us the only recent mounting of the play that treated the play as though it were all of a piece. If Shylock is the hero, then the Venetians must be villains. And so they were.

But we are confronted now with the most disturbing evidence of all: that the persistent, humane effort to read sentiment into Shylock, even when that sentiment is actually achieved, does nothing to stabilize or illuminate the play as a whole; it merely succeeds in turning it upside down.

The late Frederick Valk, for instance, created a moneylender who was expansive, genial, even generous, and he was both believable and moving so long as the rest of Tyrone Guthrie's Venice was plainly in the wrong. The fact that Antonio, Bassanio, Portia, Lorenzo, and Jessica were in the wrong, however, effectively robbed us of any interest in their love affairs. Having watched them revile a decent man and drive him sobbing from the stage, we were disinclined to indulge them their lyrical fifth act; little patience was left for polite prattle about starry nights, forfeited rings, and the conjugal bed. Shylock appears in only five of the play's twenty scenes, with a sixth devoted exclusively to conversation about him. Three-fourths of the evening, then, and all of the major characters but one, had turned slightly sour.

This new, nervous imbalance—both of structure and of sympathy for the people at hand—is not always so marked as it was in Guthrie's uncompromising production. Most productions compromise, straining for the maximum dignity and tragic emotion in Shylock while straining for the maximum gaiety in the revels of his enemies. The effect, and we have been able to see at least six such *Merchants* in the past five or six years, is always disturbing. Shylock may have seemed dignified indeed in his exchange with the judge, only to flounder miserably, immediately thereafter, in the necessary but extremely undignified business of whetting his knife on his shoe. The line "I had it of Leah . . ." may have bolted from its context with stunning sentiment; but we are fretfully aware that the line has been isolated from its context, that the actor has most carefully suppressed the frighteningly comic touches on either side of it. Even in his own scenes, quite apart from his relationship to the light nonsense at Belmont, Shylock is inconsistent, unsettling. We come away complaining of one thing or another: the actor has not been able to sustain Shylock's tragic greatness, the other players have not been adroit enough to hoist the light scenes into the air, the director has failed to pull the "two tones" of the play into satisfactory balance. After three, or six, or a dozen such productions, we reluctantly come to one of two possible conclusions: either Shakespeare never meant Shylock to be played so sympathetically, in which case he probably *was* anti-Semitic; or he did mean him to be sympathetic in the midst of all this foolery, in which case he was quite a clumsy playwright.

Both views, in effect, abandon the play. Those who come to the former conclusion simply refuse it performance, as certain high school and community theaters have done in recent years. Those who arrive at the latter conclusion go on patiently waiting for the superbly serious Shylock who is sure to come, while granting that, in the over-all management of the play, Shakespeare had temporarily lost command of his craft.

Since most of us are not quite willing to surrender the work, since there is so much in it that is irresistibly appealing, since Shylock himself will never stop teasing us, it is surprising that we have not had the energy to cast about for still another alternative—especially since one exists. There is always the hypothetical possibility that Shakespeare knew what he was doing, that what he was doing was writing a true comedy, and that he was able to sustain his single tone perfectly because in Shylock he had drawn neither a melodramatic villain nor a tragic hero but a true comic giant.

That the alternative exists, and ought to tempt us to experimentation, is plain enough. The play has always been called a comedy: it is so listed in the First Folio and in Francis Meres's catalogue of 1598. It was written circa 1596, not during the later period that produced the mixed tone of the "dark comedies," but somewhere between *A Midsummer Night's Dream* and *Much Ado About Nothing.* The oldest acting tradition has always held that, as John Munro reminds us in *The London Shakespeare,* "Shylock was apparently meant originally to be a ludicrous figure with a large nose and odd gestures which were mimicked by Launcelot." The tradition extended beyond Shakespeare's time: in his *Comic Characters of Shakespeare,* John Palmer insists that "Shylock as a comic character held the stage for over a century." The first known production after the Restoration, in 1701, featured the best-known comedian of the day, Thomas Doggett, in the role.

Indeed, there is no indication that Shylock was ever imagined as other than a comic figure until the revolutionary performance given by Charles Macklin in 1741. Whether Macklin made him a bloodcurdling villain (during the knife-whetting scene, reported a member of the audience, "Mr. Macklin was so highly characteristic in the part, that a young man who was in the pit fainted away") or a mixture of melodrama and pathos ("This is the Jew/That Shakespeare drew" enthused Pope) is not certain. What is certain is that Macklin shattered the earlier tradition and paved the way for the somber, or at least sober, Shylock we elaborate today. Macklin "rescued Shylock from the crudities of the low comedian" is Phyllis Hartnoll's verdict in *The Oxford Companion to the Theatre.*

Perhaps so. But there is something faulty in the rescue work: both character and play continue to prove troublesome and unresolved. Is it possible that the way Shylock was played in Shakespeare's time, and for nearly one hundred and fifty years thereafter, is the right way, the only practical way if the piece as a whole is to prove satisfying?

The thought horrifies us. Are we going to make Shylock a villain again and poke crude fun at him besides? Are we really prepared to double the offense we may give to Jews in the audience, while we confirm, in spades, Shakespeare's suspected anti-Semitism? The promised spectacle of a "ludicrous figure with a large nose" dancing grotesquely about the stage so that Portia and Antonio can go scot-free and the play become a unified piece of comic writing, so revolts us that we avert our eyes and cut our contemplation short.

But we have, in our quick dismay, neglected to ask certain obvious questions. What makes us think that the original comedy performance was a *low* comedy performance? Who played the part?

Not one of the low comedians, if the conjectural cast lists worked out by T. W. Baldwin can be accepted as reasonably accurate. The company's principal clowns—Kemp and Cowley—were occupied elsewhere: Kemp as Launcelot, Cowley as Old Gobbo. What sort of actor was left, then, for a funny Shylock? Apparently our Jew was the property of one Thomas Pope, creator of a quite different species of fool: Falstaff, Sir Toby Belch, Jaques, Benedick, Mercutio.

The line of parts is interesting. Thomas Pope would seem, on the face of it, to have been a comedian, most probably a superb one; and his particular humorous vein must have been capable of absorbing some fascinating complexities: a streak of knavery, a streak of melancholy, a flash of fire. One other quality leaps out of the line: the parts are one and all, no matter what skulduggery they may embrace, sympathetic. In these hands Shylock is not likely ever to have been a simple, despicable buffoon.

Even so, the likelihood that Shylock was once one of a certain brotherhood of outsize, attractive rogues does not wholly clarify the man for us. Neither Falstaff nor Jaques is really Shylock; we still lack a precise, practical, playable image, the sort of image that might have come into Shakespeare's head through a hint in his sources or in one or another comic convention of the Elizabethan stage.

The supposed sources for the play suggest very little along this line. The story of the bond appears in very early folklore, when the holder of the bond was not yet a Jew, but the atmosphere of the legends is essentially melodramatic. The Jew, the bond, the passionate love for a lady of Belmont, the lady's disguise in a court of law, and the forfeited betrothal ring are found in combination as early as 1378, in Fiorentino's *Il Pecorone;* but a translation of this work was probably not available to Shakespeare, and he is thought to have picked up the outline by hearsay, without a specific tone attached. The commercial popularity of Marlowe's *Jew of Malta* may have induced Shakespeare to write his play; but the play he wrote and the Jew he created bear only the most superficial resemblance to Marlowe's savage inventions.

These sources, which Shakespeare may have carved up and recombined in his characteristic fashion, might very well lead us to a violent Jew, a voracious Jew—but not to any comic Jew that Thomas Pope is apt to have played. Was there *no* familiar image, no elderly, moneygrubbing, fantastically funny fellow, *anywhere* in the Elizabethan storehouse to help set Shakespeare in motion and the rest of us on a likely scent?

There was such an image, just such a fellow. His name was Pantalone, and he appeared endlessly, with many droll variations but with a few indispensable comic trade-marks, in the improvised performances of the Italian *commedia dell' arte.* (The players improvised from standard scenarios, many of which survive.) That Shakespeare and his associates knew Pantalone and his retinue is quite clear. *Commedia* troupes began visiting London as early as 1574. Companies returned at intervals thereafter; one is thought to have spent the entire season in London during the year of Shakespeare's arrival from Stratford. Playwrights Thomas Heywood, Thomas Kyd, and Ben Jonson all mention these *farceurs,* with their repertory of Harlequins, Dottores, and—in the Anglicized spelling—Pantaloons. Among the papers left by Burbage's greatest actor-rival, Edward Alleyn, were four

In this century E. H. Sothern (left) and George Arliss (center) both played Shylock in the old "heavy" style. But in 1955 the late Frederick Valk (above) made of him a warm, tragic hero.

commedia scenarios, in the oldest of which *Panteloun* appears. Shakespeare himself, of course, made reference to this salty, drooling, somehow venerable figure in *As You Like It*, and elsewhere came to call his own fools "zanies," after the *zanni* of the Italian travelers. Pantalone was, as a suggestive theatrical image, available.

Who was he, what was he like? To begin with, he was a merchant of Venice. He was old, wealthy, and had his fortune tied up in shipping. When one of his cargoes was destroyed by storm or pirates, he tore his beard and spat into the sea in impotent rage. He was a miser.

"All his life long," as Pierre Louis Duchartre reconstructs him for us, "he has been engaged in trade, and he has become so sensitive to the value of money that he is an abject slave to it." His precious ducats are eternally on his mind. He is swiftly suspicious, sure that someone is going to swindle him. To help save ducats, he starves his servants. His hungry valet frequently threatens to leave him. The old father of the hungry valet sometimes comes to intercede for his son. The valet invariably mimics his master's speech, behind his back.

Pantalone has a daughter, with whom he is severe. She is an ingénue in love, eager for marriage, more eager still to be out of her father's tyrannically run household. Secretly she makes arrangements to meet her lover, usually by means of letters smuggled out by the friendly, conniving servant. When the chance comes, she elopes, often taking a supply of ducats along with her. Pantalone boils in rage, driven nearly out of his wits by his daughter's behavior. Others are delighted to see him so beset, he is such a "skinflint" and "calamity-howler."

At the last, Pantalone is the butt of the joke—robbed of his ducats, deceived by his daughter, the sputtering, breast-beating, hair-tearing victim of his own greed.

He carries, of course, a large purse at his belt. He also carries a sizable dagger. He is quick to draw and brandish the dagger when outraged, which is rather often; somehow or other, though, he is never permitted to use it. Vocally, to take a cue directly from Shakespeare, "his big manly voice, turning again toward childish treble, pipes and whistles in his sound." This shrill, shuffling, furiously gesticulating patriarch is only an inch or two shy of senility. For clothing, he wears a long black cloak, a rounded black cap, and either soft slippers or Turkish sandals. He has a prominent hooked nose.

In the *commedia* scenarios and eyewitness reports that survive, Pantalone has still other characteristics. Sometimes, for instance, he is an amorous old fool bent on marrying again, a trait that Molière took hold of and elaborated brilliantly in several of his finest comedies. In the process of making varied use of the Pantalone figure, however, Molière did not neglect the particular bundle of crotchets, nor the precise story line, we have just been describing. One of his masterpieces, *The Miser*, presents us with a greedy, near-senile Pantalone (Harpagon) whose daughter deceives him, whose servants groan over the food allotted them and helpfully conspire with the daughter, whose money is stolen, and whose comeuppance is the result of his own greed. No one questions the derivation of Harpagon from Pantalone; we have simply neglected, I think, to draw the same conclusions from the same materials in the case of Shylock.*

While it is unlikely now that anyone will ever be able to *prove* that Shakespeare took his Shylock from his memory of Pantalone, the catalogue of similarities is too striking to be dismissed. As will be obvious, each item in the catalogue appears—with a surprising minimum of alteration—in *The Merchant of Venice*. Nor do the resemblances end with the character of Shylock; through Jessica, Launcelot, Old Gobbo, and possibly Tubal, they extend to the general personnel, the incidental comic episodes, and the romantic story line of the play. When bound with the casket sequences and the lyric fifth act, these touches become part of a consistent

Since putting these comments into type, I have discovered that Professor John Robert Moore of Indiana University has drawn from some of the same hints some of the same answers.

light-comedy pattern, notes struck in a single true chord.

We might add, speculatively, that the chord itself—Shakespeare's image of Venice and all that might pass in it—may have come from his experience of watching the Italian troupes play; these *were* Italian, they *knew* Venice, they exuded its spirit in a style that was both mocking and accurate; they constituted Shakespeare's most intimate, direct, and reliable sense of the atmosphere of the Rialto.

Pantalone does suggest Shylock, just as the standard *commedia* story of a charming ingénue who outwits her foolish, niggardly father suggests at least one of the plot lines and much of the atmosphere of the play as a whole. But does Shylock suggest Pantalone? Going back to the text with these performance images in mind, does Shylock *read* as a comic, garrulous, sputtering, excitable, stingy old goat?

We have tried so hard to read the lines in every other conceivable way that fresh hearing, uncluttered by prejudicial associations, is next to impossible. But let's make the effort. Shylock is introduced this way:

Shylock. Three thousand ducats: well.

Bassanio. Ay, sir, for three months.

Shylock. For three months: well.

Bassanio. For the which, as I told you, Antonio shall be bound.

Shylock. Antonio shall become bound: well.

What are those repetitions all about? What is that rhythmic "well" doing there? Don't they sound, on quick acquaintance, like the mumbling, lip-smacking, beard-moistening reiterations of the amusingly aged? Abstracted from their context they might do as a pattern for a vaudeville routine, that familiar one in which the blear-eyed comic gropingly reiterates the instructions his straight-man is giving him until he is ready for the surprise switch. In the context of the play, they create precisely the kind of comic rhythm that lends itself to burlesque imitation by one of the secondary fools—which, of course, is what Launcelot Gobbo takes advantage of a little later in the evening. Indeed, if Launcelot's mimicry is to be effective, the initial rhythm—and the actor's management of it—must be inherently funny.

The longer speeches into which Shylock soon plunges are marked by absurd pedantry (he is constantly explaining what is already clear), further chatterbox repetition, and the device of a long list of negatives swiftly followed by a simple, complacent positive. The devices are all stock equipment for the comedian. Shylock has, in addition, a leering sense of humor of his own; he rather fancies himself as a jokester, doing his best to make a merry jest of the bond itself and indulging himself in casual throwaways (asked if his money has the potency of ewes and rams, he murmurs "I cannot tell. I make it breed as fast"). It is not difficult, here, to recognize the bland, obsequious humor of the man who thinks himself cleverer than anyone else, who rubs his palms and chuckles happily as he spreads molasses for the flies and thinks lovingly of the future; he is at once crafty and transparent, a combination calculated to make him comic.

The next we hear of Shylock we hear from his hungry servant Launcelot ("I am famished in his service. You may tell every finger I have with my ribs") and from his put-upon daughter ("Our house is hell"). The material is unmistakably giddy, topped by a romantic letter secretly delivered by the conniving servant; Shylock's household is established by a stand-up clown improvising pure nonsense.

When Shylock himself appears a scene later, the Pantalone-like stinginess recurs as he washes his hands of his servant (who was "a huge feeder"), the senile pedantry returns as he gives Jessica instructions for the night ("stop my house's ears, I mean my casements"). The phrase "I did dream of money-bags tonight" is so blatantly grotesque in its wording that it cannot be anything other than a cartoon of avarice. There are also three basic comedy bits in the scene: the business of Shylock's being of two minds, shouting for Jessica below a window and pursuing a completely different thought at the same time; the business of the shout being echoed, unexpectedly, by a too-helpful servant, startling Shylock and causing him to turn on the servant; the business of Shylock's not quite hearing a sly exchange between the servant and his daughter, leading Shylock to ask what was said and Jessica to misreport it. Add to this the fact that Launcelot and Jessica are, throughout the scene, playing *against* Shylock's abstracted, slightly frantic mood, punctuating his scattered instructions with puns, irrelevancies, malapropisms, and—we may suppose—sly winks.

Once Jessica and the ducats are gone, we do not immediately see Shylock in his anguish. The anguish is reported to us—in itself a suggestion that it is going to be humorously handled—and reported to us not by fellow Jews who might view Shylock's plight sympathetically but by friends of Bassanio's who can only view it with comic relish. Is the report truly comic? Why does it not strike all actors—as it does almost all audiences—that "my ducats, and my daughter!" is a roaring incongruity, a pairing of values so mismatched that their juxtaposition seems the very soul of comedy? If one or another value gains a little edge in importance as the harangue goes on, it is the ducats and not the daughter—the scales fall not toward sentiment but toward the absurd. And the incongruity is stressed in that splendid burst of incoherence, "O my Christian ducats!" As Solanio says of it, "I never heard a passion so confused."

What of the scene in which we *do* meet the ravaged Shylock? Its structure, after the introductory exchange between Shylock and Bassanio's friends, is completely, explicitly comic. Even the introductory passage has its familiar echoes, the obtuse and literal overexplanation ("I say, my daughter is my flesh and my blood"), the monomaniac repetitions ("Let him look to his bond"); even the "Hath not a Jew eyes?" speech begins with one of Shylock's snappish jokes (asked what Antonio's flesh is good for, he raps out "To bait fish withal"). But here is what happens in the scene proper.

Tubal informs Shylock that Jessica cannot be found. Shylock is at once in the abyss, wallowing in those same comic incongruities Solanio found so "outrageous" ("I would my daughter were dead at my foot, and the jewels in her ear!") Tubal next reports that Antonio has had ill luck. Shylock ("What, what, what?") is swiftly transported to seventh heaven ("Good news, good news! Ha, ha!") Tubal mentions that Jessica is thought to have spent fourscore ducats in one night. Shylock dives to despair. Tubal speaks of Antonio's creditors. Shylock soars. Tubal speaks of a ring Jessica has traded for a monkey. Shylock writhes in torment. Tubal remarks that Antonio is undone. Shylock bursts into a fever of delighted activity.

Up down, up down, with the sentences growing tighter, the exhilaration and the agony coming closer together, Shylock is alternately sobbing and gleeful in ever faster reversals until he is all but spun off the stage. The trick remains, of course, standard property among comedians today.

As we move toward the courtroom, Shylock's frenzied bout with Antonio and his jailer is a kind of popped-corn rehash of all the repetitions, rationalizations, and caterwaulings we've by now become accustomed to. And, in briefly renewing our acquaintance with Jessica, we are given a significant scene which is now most often omitted in production: a lively, witty, playful, extraordinarily candid passage in which the entire Jewish-Christian theme is made light-hearted sport of ("This making of Christians will raise the price of hogs"). The scene is delightfully in keeping so long as the play is regarded as a thoroughgoing comedy; it is normally abandoned in our own mountings, I suppose, because the mountings themselves make it inexplicable.

In the courtroom Shylock is impudent to the judge, fawning with Portia, shrill in his glee over "A Daniel come to judgment," filled with a wonderfully pious righteousness ("Shall I lay perjury upon my soul? No, not for Venice"), whimpering when defeated ("Shall I not have barely my principal?"), and protected in tone at every turn by Portia's own little jokes and Gratiano's ebullience. Through it all, he whets his knife on his shoe, gleefully anticipating the victory to come, sassing the Duke who bids him to desist. That this business is irretrievably funny may be best attested to by every actor who has tried to play it as though it were not. The image is, simply as an image, outrageously, preposterously ludicrous; in ever so sober a production the snickers cannot be stilled. It is possible that Shakespeare, who knew a comedy bit when he saw one, did not intend embarrassed snickers but wholehearted belly laughs.

These are the devices that the part and the play are made of, the comic carpentry on which both structures rest. Let us suppose that Shylock *could* be played as a delightful dervish of a Pantalone, and that the comedy as a whole would profit by the vision. Clearly, we have not yet accounted for everything. Though the "Hath not a Jew eyes?" passage begins in a joke, it moves on to something else; to a quite firm defense of Jewishness and the common humanity of Jews and Christians. Though the "Leah" line is surrounded by comic images, it is in itself instantly moving, a catch of breath in the middle of a laugh. If Shylock is the English cousin of an Italian vaudevillian, where does that pathos come from? Precisely where it has always come from, I think: from that unexpected stab of sorrow that so often accompanies the comic image when it is raised to its highest power.

The likelihood that pathos will emerge from the most outlandishly, even grotesquely, conceived cartoon stems from a very simple principle: all truly funny figures are necessarily sympathetic figures. If a man makes us laugh, we like him. He may do quite terrible things in pursuit of the objects of his lust, his avarice, or his spite; because he delights us in his outlandishness, in his methods, in his mania—and because we are quite sure he is going to be as delightfully discomfited—we feel no emotional revulsion for the things he

A standard character in the Italian commedia dell' arte is the Venetian merchant Pantalone. In this seventeenth-century etching by Jacques Callot he needs only a purse and a knife to be the image of Shylock.

does, or for his person. We secretly admire him; we look forward eagerly to his next appearance on stage; in an oddly inverted but very understanding way, we feel for him. And because we feel for this enchanted buffoon, we can always be, delicately, touched by him. It is perfectly clear to us that Chaplin can kick a child at one moment and involve us emotionally at the next. (I recently took my wife to a revival of an early Chaplin film; her response at the end was "Why do you say it's funny? *I* cried!") Yet the dominant Chaplin image is funny; the pathos wouldn't stir if it weren't.

A considerable complexity is required of any comic figure if so sobering a note is to be embraced, and to be embraced without destroying the dominant image. That the original Pantalone is capable of nearly infinite extension and very rich variation is amply demonstrated by Molière; we do not have to look to Shakespeare alone to find it. Molière's Harpagon (*The Miser*) and Arnolphe (*The School for Wives*) are both Pantalones, closely derived from the *commedia* form; and they are both, in Molière's hands, men of vast stature and psychological subtlety. Nor can any villainy they may do force us to despise them. Indeed Arnolphe comes at last, in *his* up-and-down torment between raging anger and tender devotion, to a note of brokenhearted submission:

"You want to see me weep? And beat my breast?
You want to have me tear out half my hair?
Or shall I kill myself? Is that what you want?
Oh, cruel girl, I'm ready to prove it so." *

That last line is no longer quite comedy; it is Arnolphe's way of saying "Hath not an old, ugly man the power to love?" But Molière pulls him back quickly from this hint of a heart; the note is only faintly struck; Molière's characteristic tone, even when his characters are at their most complex, is one of detachment.

Not so Shakespeare's. Shakespeare is at his most characteristic, in dealing with outsize buffoons, in his management of Falstaff. Falstaff is a coward, a bully, a liar, a lecher, a tosspot. And he can be hurt, hurt so badly that it hastens his death. When we at last ask what was the special contribution of Shakespeare's genius to the tangle of sources that might have given birth to any such character, we can answer: the power of introducing strong feeling into the most Rabelaisian of rogues without breaking the mold that made him essentially merry. There is no reason to suppose that he might not have been able to do the same thing, with the assistance of the same actor, for Shylock.

If we are to imagine Pantalone as a playing model for Shylock, then we are not obliged to stop at the simple, playful level of senile rhythms and servant-slapping horseplay; we are free to imagine Pantalone risen to the complex comic stature and psychological brilliance of the best worst man in Molière; and we are further free to see in him the levels of sentiment that Shakespeare divined in the biggest boozers and most brazen scalawags he knew. It's a tall order, and one that has not been delivered in more than two hundred

*Morris Bishop's translation

years. Ralph Richardson might bring it off. The Bert Lahr of *Waiting for Godot* might just possibly make it stick.

What of the Jewishness? Pantalone, with his black cloak, black cap, and exceedingly prominent nose, was not Jewish. In the process of dovetailing sources, Shakespeare can have taken the Jewishness from the *Il Pecorone* tradition, from the commercial popularity of Marlowe's play, from the talk current in London after Lopez's execution. Wherever he took it, what he took was a stereotype: the medieval stereotype of the Jew as avaricious. He took it *as* a stereotype; there were too few Jews then living in England for Shakespeare to have had extensive personal knowledge of the race. Insofar as he borrowed the stereotype at all, and he probably borrowed it for commercial reasons, he cannot be absolved of a certain opportunism, of having lent himself to the exploitation and perpetuation of a disparaging legend. (He behaved even more badly, and for just as poor reasons, toward Richard III.) The fact in itself is unpleasant, and we will have to live with it.

We had best, however, not be smug about the matter. It should first be remembered that Shakespeare would have employed the stereotype as matter-of-factly, and with as little malice, as an American playwright of the early twentieth century making uncritical and even affectionate use of those other stereotypes, the superstitious Negro and the drunken Irishman. Furthermore, Shakespeare might have treated his borrowed equation in one of two ways. He might have made the Jew a bloodcurdling melodramatic villain, as most of his sources had done. Or he might have taken the kinder course and made him comic, which is what I think he did do. In the public mind, the progress of social adjustment moves something like this: from the alien as menace to the alien as buffoon to the alien as human being. It is quite conceivable that Shakespeare actually furthered understanding by nudging this process into its second stage. I do not say that he did this deliberately; but he had noticed that a Jew—and especially a funny Jew—had eyes. If we can imagine an accepted stereotype slowly and mysteriously taking on, under its manipulator's instincts, a broad and rather affectionate grin—as the superstitious Negro did when Mark Twain got around to Nigger Jim, or, more pertinently, as the drunken Irishman did when Sean O'Casey decided to make us fond of the loutish Captain Boyle—we may have come closer to measuring Shakespeare's peculiar achievement, and to the image in his mind as well. The Shylock we find on our stages is ambiguous, nervous, not very attractive in spite of his tears; Shakespeare's Shylock—if he was as funny as the earliest tradition tells us he was and as Thomas Pope might well have made him—may easily have been more likable.

The illustration at the beginning of the text, by the way, is not a drawing of Shylock, but of Pantalone.

Walter Kerr, drama critic of the New York Herald Tribune, *wrote the article on new theaters in the July, 1959,* HORIZON.

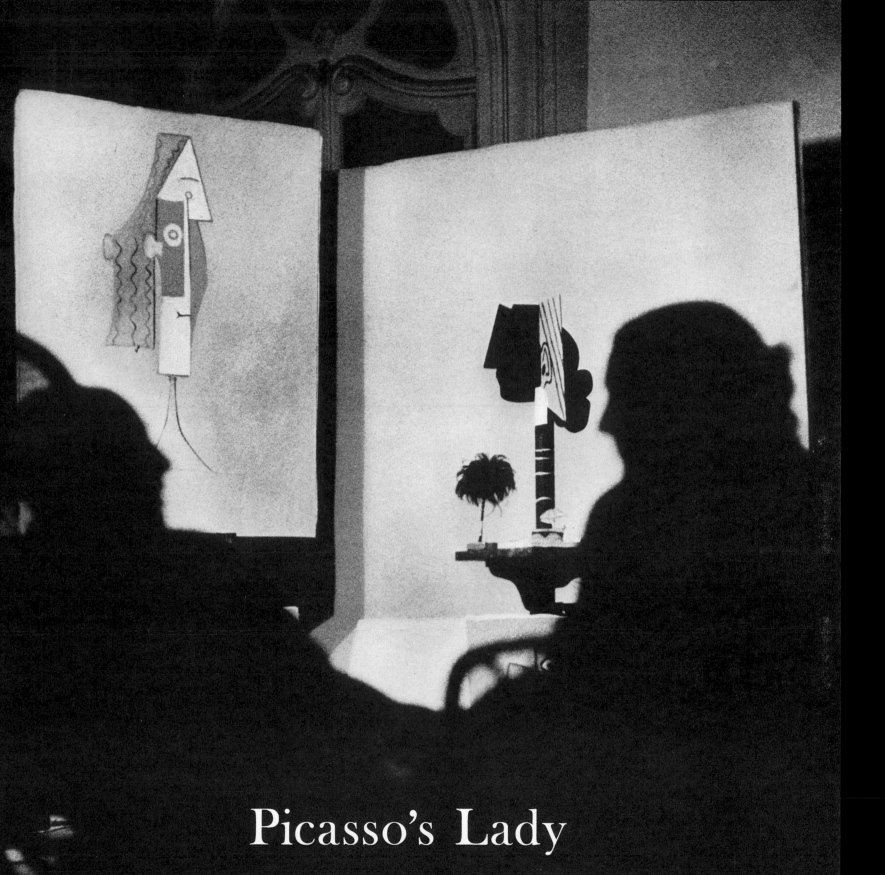

Picasso's Lady

The profile of Jacqueline Roque, seen in silhouette beside the

artist, may become classic in art history. On the next pages:

Picasso's recent paintings of her in his own collection and

their story. Photographs and text by David Douglas Duncan

Ever since 1954, visitors to the home of Pablo Picasso on the French Riviera have been greeted by a serenely beautiful young woman of exceptional charm. Most of these guests have left the famous artist's villa carrying with them memories of her nearly as vivid as their impressions of the Maestro himself. Much of the warmth and hospitality reflected by the painter's studio-home seemed to flow from this girl. Her name is Jacqueline Roque. She has shared Picasso's life and has been beside him constantly for the past six years.

Numerous experts on today's art firmly believe that much of the vigor and gaiety of Picasso's work of these same six years is directly attributable to Jacqueline, who is his everyday companion, model for most of his latest portraits, confidante with whom everything is shared, hostess at his table, and perhaps the most loving person ever to enter his life. Every thought, every act of her life is dedicated to making Picasso happy and to providing him with the maximum of freedom from interruptions so that he may work to his heart's content. Those who enjoy Picasso's work owe a great deal to Jacqueline. She has added immeasurably to the environment in which this modern master has been most productive.

Picasso is Spanish, and seventy-eight. Jacqueline is French, and just over thirty. Despite the vast difference in their ages the visitor to their home is immediately impressed by an overwhelming fact: these two people are ideally matched. No barrier separates them. Of all the lifelong friends and admirers who swirl around Picasso—poets, bullfighters, other painters, actors, writers, museum directors, and art collectors—it is only Jacqueline who truly mirrors the artist's thoughts. Her face reflects his face and feelings to a remarkable degree, even though she may not be looking at him at all. When he smiles, she smiles. When he is pensive, so is Jacqueline. When he questions someone with his eyes, her eyes search for answers. When he daydreams, she is motionless, utterly quiet, lost in thought.

Among Jacqueline's many roles in Picasso's life is that of diplomat. There are times when visitors come hoping to purchase paintings straight from the studio. Picasso's acute distaste for such negotiations is well known. Some collectors, probably stunned by the incredible mass of Picassos against the walls and underfoot, still attempt a purchase by trying to corner Jacqueline in their plan to bargain with Picasso. Her response is always a polite but extremely firm "No!" Such affairs are handled by his Paris dealer, never in the studio. Nothing is for sale. The works seen around the studio are viewed much like his own children—and loved almost as well.

Picasso is without doubt one of the hardest-working men, in any art or craft, living today. His energy is boundless, as is his imagination. When even the latest of Côte d'Azur night spots close their doors, Picasso's studio lights are usually still burning, for it is late at night that he does most of his work. Jacqueline always waits with him, and for him. Her knowledge of painting is vast, as is her memory of specific canvases—either by his hand or that of any other master. She is one of the very few people with whom Picasso will discuss the technique of painting. She is the model for many of his portraits,

TEXT CONTINUED ON PAGE 104

Of Jacqueline de Vauvenargues, *David Douglas Duncan writes: "Picasso painted this small canvas early in the spring of 1959, when he moved into the great Chateau de Vauvenargues in the south of France, near Aix-en-Provence. He placed the portrait over the fireplace in the room which he had converted into a studio. He told me, laughingly, that the old-time knights had had their heraldic crests for their castles— so now he had one, too. Later, when revisiting Vauvenargues, I asked about this canvas, for it had disappeared from the studio. Picasso tried to shush me, but Jacqueline had already heard my question and exploded, 'You can't imagine what he did!' Naturally I asked. It seems that Picasso, one day while wandering around the studio, picked the portrait off the mantelpiece and completely repainted it. Jacqueline de Vauvenargues was gone. At that moment Jacqueline herself walked into the studio. Seeing what Picasso had done, she burst into tears. Distressed by her distress, he took out his handkerchief and wiped away all of the fresh paint, and the original portrait reappeared. Picasso told me, 'Jacqueline was crying—so was I, the paint kept coming off, and JACQUELINE DE VAUVENARGUES started to come out, just like developing a photograph. It was wonderful!' The portrait now sits atop the mantelpiece in Jacqueline's bedroom, where she placed it after rescuing it from Picasso."*

At top: Jacqueline Roque wears a ceramic necklace Picasso made for her. Above: His littered studio in Cannes, where many of her portraits were painted, including the very first one, hanging on the center wall. In color: Four 1959 portraits of her. In that at bottom left, she is in the corner.

The Short and Vivid Life

Mr. Duncan recalls: *"Soon after Picasso and Jacqueline moved into the chateau of Vauvenargues I passed by to visit and saw all of his latest works. Among them was a portrait of Jacqueline painted in sweeping black slashes against a scarlet sky [above]. I asked for permission to photograph it together with the other new canvases. Several weeks later I called again, bring-*

of a Picasso Painting

...ng a slide projector with which we could view the color shots I'd made. We turned the projector ...gainst the dining room wall. When I got to this painting Picasso asked that I leave it on the wall ...or a longer time than the others. 'It's only a memory now,' he said with a grunt. For he had since ...verpainted all of it save Jacqueline's own image and evolved a quite different canvas [above]."

TEXT CONTINUED FROM PAGE 98

yet she never sits before his easel. He paints her from memory, or, while she sits beside him, he takes sheet iron and tubular steel and makes profiles which are amazingly like Jacqueline herself (see the photograph on page 97).

Like other men, Picasso is almost helpless when the woman of his life turns on the charm to get his approval for something she desires. When she is successful, Picasso just laughs—and goes back to his work. There is much gaiety and laughter around Picasso's home. I remember a day in summer—and it was typical—when Paolo, Picasso's son, tried to pour coffee into Jacqueline's beach slacks. Picasso, eyes glowing, let her defend herself. Later, as she brought him something special from the table, she threw an affectionate hammer lock around his head—like a wrestler. We were eating in the kitchen, as usual. Picasso often says that the kitchen is the heart of the home, any home, and it is his favorite place to eat. Three dogs—dachshund, boxer, and Dalmatian—tumble between his and Jacqueline's feet, competing for choice morsels handed down from the table above. A bright green frog sits in its jar near the stove hopefully peering through bulging golden eyes at the man and girl who take turns catching wandering flies for its dinner.

Picasso and Jacqueline live an almost frugal existence together. She rarely leaves the house without him, and then only to market or shop. The studio is almost bare of "modern" comforts, with few pieces of furniture, no curtains, unmatched plates and silver service; yet it is a fabulous place in every respect. It is bursting with creations of Picasso's mind and hands. Paintings, sculpture, bronzes, ceramics, lithographs, sketches, drawings, etchings, engravings, pets and children, guests and old friends, who possess some of the most famous names in their professions or arts, all congregate in the studio—when the door is open. There probably isn't another house like it on earth. Picasso's magic has made it possible—but Jacqueline's love has added a final glow.

David Douglas Duncan, the well-known photographer, recently published The Private World of Pablo Picasso, *an intimate album of the painter's life.*

Right: The veteran of half a century's fabulous life in art embraces the companion of his seventies. Below: The painter adds a fixed installation to his house. On acquiring the remote fifteenth-century chateau of Vauvenargues last year, Picasso installed plumbing, electricity, and a modern kitchen but did not end his improvements there. To enliven Jacqueline's huge bathroom he painted a mural of which a key figure is this faun playing his pipes for the bather.

Lytton Strachey's mordant approach set a new style in biography—now somewhat in disfavor

A PROPOSAL OF MARRIAGE

The time was only fifty years ago, the place Fitzroy Square in the Blooms-bury district of London, hard by the British Museum. It has gone shabby now, but then it housed the beginnings of one of those brilliant if self-con-scious groups which so often blow up literary and artistic storms. This one, the Bloomsbury Group, was not merely whitecaps in a teacup, it turned out later; its influence still eddies about us. At its center sat the shy, aloof, and fiercely intellectual Virginia Stephen, and there came courting, if you could call it that, a clever but rather bloodless young man from Cambridge, Lytton Strachey. She was twenty-seven in 1909, and he twenty-nine; none of her novels was published yet, and none of his biographies, but they fairly ran over with bright talk of books and writers. Strachey would explore his inner soul in a stream of letters, often in quite passionate, if enigmatic terms. She was more reserved, but encouragingly chatty. It was write, write, write, and—occasionally—tea. Once she left her glove at his house, although it is hard to suspect her of deliberately employing so ancient a maneuver. He wrote at once:

So shocking! Your glove appeared the moment you'd left the house. I'm afraid you must have shivered without it. I've just finished my solitary dinner . . . and now I've settled down for the evening before my gas fire, surrounded by my Maintenon and the Dictionary of National Biography. . . . If I could have my way, I should go out to dinner every night, and then to a party or an opera, and then I should have a champagne supper, and then I should go to bed in some won-derful person's arms. Wouldn't you? When one reflects on one's pallid existence one shudders. But I suppose there are always the triumphs of Art.

He seemed always to be snuffling with unromantic colds, though he could write boldly about himself as a "wild man of the woods." She thought of him, rather, she said, as "an oriental potentate in a flowered dressing gown." One day, however, the wild potentate let all this giddy talk give way for a moment to action. What happened is best described by Strachey himself, writing later to his brother:

I had a decided reverse the other day . . . I proposed to Virginia and was ac-cepted. It was an awkward moment, as you may imagine, especially as I realized, the very minute it was happening, that the whole thing was repulsive to me. Her sense was amazing, and luckily, it turned out that she's not in love. The result was that I was able to manage a fairly honourable retreat.

What Virginia Stephen thought that day when passion blundered into the room and then stumbled out is not recorded. Decades later, the mood of it becomes believable if one inspects Henry Lamb's painting of the author of *Eminent Victorians* (left) in his guise of Georgian aesthete. It was done not long after Miss Stephen received a more durable proposal and announced it to her stringy ex-suitor thus:

Ha! Ha!
Virginia Stephen
Leonard Woolf
6th June, 1912

Virginia Woolf's flickering wit and lumi-nous mind attracted not only Strachey but E. M. Forster, Clive and Vanessa Bell (her sister), John Maynard Keynes, and her brilliant husband, Leonard Woolf. She was a master of the essay and her innovations added new dimensions to the English novel in such works as Mrs. Dal-loway *and* To the Lighthouse. *She died tragically, by her own hand, in 1941.*

By OLIVER JENSEN

AN INTRODUCTION

Peter Quennell was still a schoolboy when Lytton Strachey and Virginia Woolf (preceding page) achieved renown soon after the First World War. Yet in 1922, when only seventeen, Quennell attained early celebrity of his own by appearing in the distinguished anthology *Georgian Poetry* in company with such stars as Edmund Blunden, Walter de la Mare, D. H. Lawrence, and Robert Graves. Later the young poet branched out into other forms of writing and became one of the leading biographers, cultural historians, and essayists of Britain's new generation, as well as editor of the *Cornhill Magazine* and then of *History Today*.

For a youthful talent seeking entry to the brilliant and brittle literary world of early postwar London, few doors were so magical as that of the already fabulous Edith Sitwell—glittering poet, lady of oracular intellectual bearing, and sister of the no less intellectual brothers Sacheverell and Osbert. In his reminiscences of his life in letters, soon to be published under the title *The Sign of the Fish* (Viking), Peter Quennell records the triumphant moment in 1922 when the Sitwell door was opened to him.

About this time I met Richard Hughes [the novelist who while at Oxford had published Quennell's poetry in *his* anthology, *Public School Verse*]. One summer afternoon he took me to call on Edith Sitwell, leading me along a Bayswater street and up several flights of dusky stairs, to the topmost level of a block of "mansion-flats," where we halted slightly bemused and breathless. Behind that dark uncommunicative door lay the enchanted realm I longed to enter.

Nor was my first glimpse in any way disappointing. The bell was rung; we heard an answering movement; and there upon the threshold stood the famous poetess, tall, attenuated, and elegant as one of those sculptured saints and martyrs who keep guard around the portals of Chartres. Sheathed in a garment of gold brocade, wearing a toque of gilded feathers and a large jeweled cross which, I afterwards learned, had originally belonged to Cagliostro, Miss Sitwell raised a finger to her lips—on her long pale distinguished hand were several impressive rings set with big fragments of semiprecious stone—and murmured warningly, before we advanced, that there was a madman in the room beyond. Again, I was not to be disappointed. On the end of a small sofa crouched a haggard foreign poet—the demented Northern bard, nicknamed "The Icelander," already portrayed by Osbert Sitwell in a volume of his five-fold autobiography—describing the horrible and fantastic visions that pursued him when he walked abroad, notably a band of little dark men,

In 1928 Cecil Beaton entertained the Sitwells in his London garden, and took this photograph of an improbable pas de trois: *Osbert, Sacheverell, and Edith. Were they celebrating some arcane rite of spring, or was it—could it have been—ring-around-a-rosy? The mind reels.*

By PETER QUENNELL

TO THE SITWELLS

carrying large unrolled umbrellas, who perpetually dogged his footsteps, and harried and threatened him wherever he fled. On the opposite end of the sofa perched an elderly lady, entirely clothed in black velvet, and visibly quivering with alarm beneath a wide black picture hat. Her profile was aquiline and boldly whitened, her lips were summarily painted a brilliant red; and from under the brim of her hat appeared an array of yellow Gorgonian curls. This, I subsequently discovered, was that good and charming woman, the once fashionable novelist Ada Leverson, whom her friend Oscar Wilde had christened "the Sphinx," and who had befriended him with heroic devotion while he awaited his second trial at the Old Bailey. Like many deaf people, the Sphinx enjoyed talking; but for the moment she had been reduced to silence, as the madman, with his glittering eyes, edged close to her across the sofa, and she shrank away from him against its arm, doing her best to seem attentive and making tremulous propitiatory gestures. After the humdrum quietude of my parents' house, the drama that I was witnessing appeared particularly strange and desperate. At last I had entered the literary world, in which beauty, lunacy, and genius were woven together into the pattern of everyday life.

Later, I often visited Miss Sitwell's receptions, and usually found the Sphinx attending, always dressed in the same style —rich black velvet was her only wear—and, although considerably less perturbed, seated on the same sofa. Many other visitors had climbed the stairs, including some celebrated and gifted persons—Wyndham Lewis, for example, stationed moody and pallid beside the window—as well as a numerous assemblage of country cousins and favorite lame dogs. The poetess would revive them with cupfuls of strong Indian tea and feed them upon "penny buns," to which a heavy coating of white-of-egg had given the luster of antique glazed pottery. Now and then, she would read aloud—not, however, from her own verses, but from a correspondence she was carrying on with an irritable retired soldier who lived nearby, and who kept some noisy domestic animals which frequently disturbed her hours of work. Both neighbors were of an extremely pugnacious turn; but everyone agreed that the poetess's latest retort—for she was used to disciplining editors and castigating impertinent newspaper critics—had left her miserable adversary with not a leg to stand on. Sometimes these readings were interrupted by the sudden arrival of her two brothers. They did not remain with us for very long, and generally produced the impression

of having descended from a different plane. Circling rapidly around the room, and as rapidly shaking hands, "How are *you*?" they would inquire, "And how are *you*?" placing the emphasis upon the last word, in a tone that, although kindly and courteous, did not suggest that they required an answer. Bayswater was not their natural habitat; one associated them with a delightful house in Chelsea, with evenings at the Russian Ballet, and supper parties at the "Eiffel Tower." Soon they exhausted their store of greetings in which *ave* conveyed a hint of *vale*, and by a series of swift, circuitous moves had swept back gracefully towards the door. Their fine heads, as they turned to vanish, recalled twin faces stamped on a single coin. Having embraced their sister and assumed their overcoats, they began to hurry down the stairs.

Edith, Osbert, and Sacheverell Sitwell, at the period of which I am writing, formed a solid literary phalanx, always ready to charge headlong against the monstrous array of boors and boobies. But their literary method was as eclectic as their controversial strategy, if they had been sufficiently provoked, was bellicose and straightforward. They assembled the imagery of their poems from a dozen diverse sources— from the art and architecture of Southern Europe, from the ballet and the modern stage. They loved traveling and listening to music; and their youth had been spent between an Edwardian seaside resort, from which Osbert Sitwell drew the raw material of many of his short stories, a castle among the vineyards of Tuscany, and an ancient English country house, islanded in the Derbyshire coal fields, where smuts float down from the air like snow and a delicate film of soot darkens the tree boles and gathers on the rims of the fountains and the white shoulders of Italian statues. With so broad and fruitful a province to command, they did not believe that poetic inspiration developed most prosperously beneath an English hedge; and they were apt to laugh at the rustic Georgian Poets, who seemed to pass their time sauntering and botanizing around the muddy landscape that enclosed their country cottages, picking a celandine here, and there, over a five-barred gate, holding despondent conversations "with a lonely lamb." * The flora that the Sitwells admired could not be grown in a herbaceous border; the fauna that peopled their verse was as odd as anything to be discovered in the medieval bestiaries. Asked by his commanding officer at a wartime mess whether he was not fond of cats, Osbert Sitwell had returned a resolute negative, explaining that he preferred leopards.

* "I lingered at a gate and talked/A little with a lonely lamb"
William Kerr, "Counting Sheep," *Georgian Poetry* 1920–1922

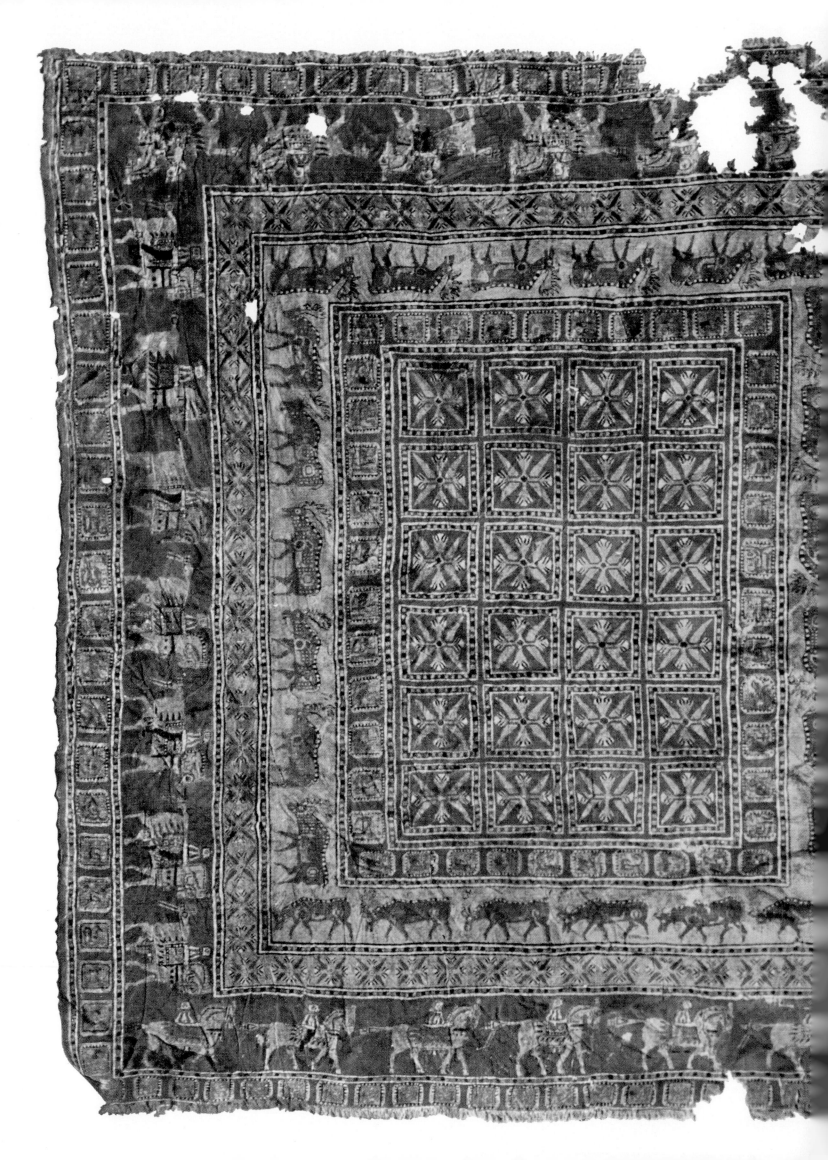

THE TROVE OF
PAZYRYK

A grave high on the Southern Siberian steppes yields up a Persian rug of phenomenal antiquity, preserved in ice for twenty-four hundred years

Some twenty-four centuries ago a band of nomads gathered at a place now known as Pazyryk, in the Altai Mountains of southern Siberia, to bury a chieftain. They laid him in a log-walled chamber cut into the earth, caparisoned in his finest robes with his treasures about him: richly embroidered hangings of felt, embossed and decorated saddles, and a splendid rug brought from a far-off land. Slaying his horses and dressing them with masks of felt, the nomads buried them in an adjoining chamber alongside a ceremonial carriage, presumably that their lord might journey fittingly to celestial lands. Then they covered the burial vault with a roof of bark and logs, and topped the grave with stones against the deprivation of robbers and the winds that lash these high steppes.

The grave was not proof against thieves, who broke into it and probably carried off the ornaments of gold which were so often buried with men of rank. But against the greater plunderers of time and rot, the funerary trove remained secure. Finally, between 1947 and 1950, as part of the extensive upsurge of Soviet archaeological activity since the Second World War, archaeologists under Professor S. I. Rudenko excavated five

Discovered by Soviet archaeologists in its subterranean deepfreeze, this wool pile carpet dates from the fifth century B.C. and measures 6 by 6½ feet. Together with other treasures found at remote Pazyryk, the rug is now in the Hermitage Museum at Leningrad.

111

FROM *Kul'tura Naseleniya Gorno-Altaya V' Skifskoe Vremya*, S. I. RUDENKO, ACADEMY OF SCIENCES OF THE U.S.S.R. 1953

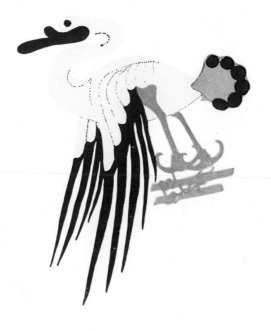

kurgans, or burial mounds, at Pazyryk. They found the contents astonishingly well-preserved by the perennial ice that filled the graves.

From the fifth *kurgan* they removed the prize, the 6 by 6½ foot wool pile carpet shown on pages 110–111. On the basis of stylistic analyses of its motifs and of those of other fabrics from the grave, Russian scholars have determined that it dates from the fifth century B.C., making it by far the oldest pile carpet known—older by two thousand years, perhaps, than the earliest Persian carpet. That the carpet is in fact Persian, Soviet archaeologists have deduced from the resemblance of its designs to those of Achaemenid Persia.

Its central field is made up of quatrefoils of Assyrian origin; this is edged by a line of griffins with turned-back heads. The next border is composed of a line of grazing stags, which bear stylized designs that are typical of Assyrian and Achaemenid Persian art: circle and comma on the shoulders, circle in brackets on the haunch, and stripe on the belly. The widest border shows a pattern of alternately mounted and dismounted horsemen. The plumed horses, tails tied up in bows, with breast collars and saddle rugs instead of saddles, are also characteristic of Achaemenid Persia. The riders in their caftans, snug breeches, boots, and headdresses look Persian or Median.

When Professor Rudenko announced his find, experts in the West were skeptical; few believed that knotted pile carpets had been made in antiquity. Since then those who have examined the Pazyryk rug are convinced that it is truly knotted, that is, not woven with a loop. Its age is accepted through the circumstances of its preservation, but certain scholars have suggested its origin as Turkish, or even Altai, although its design is based on Persian motifs.

The antiquity of this splendid relic would not alone account for the celebration it has enjoyed in the scholarly press. The Scyths, who dominated western Asia during the Achaemenid rule of Persia (550 to 330 B.C.), are known to have been nomads, but little more is known about their most northeastern branches, including the Altai tribes. The finding of a precious Persian rug in the funerary horde of a native chieftain suggests that the Altai were powerful and far-ranging traders. And additional discoveries made in the excavated burial mounds reveal other extensive contacts on the part of the Altai nomads. In *kurgan* 5 archaeologists found a beautiful Chinese silk horsecloth, together with the swans of sewn and stuffed felt that are shown at left top and bottom. If the latter were made locally, they reflect a Chinese influence.

One of the most striking finds in the same mound was an embroidered felt wall covering, nearly 12 feet high. The fantastic winged and antlered figure shown at left center is a detail from it. Professor Rudenko believes that this hanging is the work of indigenous Altai craftsmen. Such a motif is absent from Achaemenid art but occurs in that of Hittite kingdoms as early as the fourteenth century B.C., and thus suggests that the Scythian tribes of the Altai region may have had pre-Achaemenid cultural ties with western Asia.

In opening this natural Siberian deepfreeze, archaeologists are shedding light on an early culture that evidently enjoyed great vitality and widespread communications. They have also added a unique treasure to the renowned Hermitage Museum at Leningrad, where the Pazyryk finds are now displayed. One Western visitor to the museum who not long ago stopped to marvel at Professor Rudenko's rug was the wife of the Vice President of the United States.

A FABULOUS VISITOR FROM FORMOSA

*"The best man I ever knew," Dr. Johnson called him
—but that was well after George Psalmanazar had
repented of a hoax that fooled all learned England*

The Funeral, or Way of Burning the Dead Bodies

*Relying entirely upon a fertile imagination, Psalmanazar conjured up in his massive
Description of Formosa (1704) such scenes as this. He himself had never left Europe.*

In 1702 the War of the Spanish Succession was sputtering on the Continent when the
attention of George Lauder, the British major general who was governing the Dutch
town of Sluys, was attracted to a young man in one of the regiments of the Duke of
Mecklenburg.

Psalmanazar, he called himself. Although his large, dark, melancholy eyes and rose-
bud mouth had nothing of the Oriental look, he claimed to be a Japanese. The men of
his regiment reported that he had a little book with figures of the sun, moon, and stars
in it, and that these had something to do with his religion. The rest of the book was
filled, they said, with such strange writing as no one had ever seen before. Several times

Psalmanazar's Formosans wore kilts but "no Breeches"

a day Psalmanazar would open the book and chant from it.

When the men of his regiment inquired what he was up to, he would tell them strange stories of his pagan faith, which seemed to involve worship of the sun but also included the sacrifice of thousands of infants every year, back in his home country. The young man loved to dispute religious questions, and had even challenged all comers to open debate. Obviously skilled in philosophy, logic, and Latin, he usually won the argument, exposing the inconsistencies of Christian doctrine in a way that was quite alarming.

So Lauder sent for him. He also sent for a number of officers and for William Innes, the chaplain of a Scotch regiment. They talked with the young Japanese and were impressed with his learning but disturbed by his sturdy paganism. Psalmanazar suggested a public debate, which a local Calvinist minister accepted.

When Psalmanazar described the infant sacrifices demanded by his religion, the Calvinist called out in horror: "Does this not savor of cruelty in your God, that he will have men sacrificed to him?"

"Your God is yet more cruel," snapped Psalmanazar, thrusting at the Christian doctrine of predestination, "for if it be cruel to deprive men of this temporal life, though by this means they are admitted to eternal life, certainly it is infinitely more cruel to create men on purpose to make them eternally miserable and to condemn them to this misery before they are born, without any respect to the good or evil they shall do, and so to sacrifice them to the devil."

When Psalmanazar went on to tell how his god appeared in the shape of an elephant or an ox, the minister was outraged. "It is impossible that God who is omnipotent, infinite, immense, incomprehensible, and eternal could be in-

cluded in the body of such a beast," said he.

"You believe that the Holy Ghost, who is God infinite, immense, etc., did appear under the shape of a dove, which is much less than either an elephant or an ox," retorted Psalmanazar. So the argument ended.

Innes invited the young man to his lodgings, handed him a few small coins at each visit, and while pumping him for information about Japan, gradually put him at ease. Then one day, as they talked about the Japanese language, Innes handed Psalmanazar a volume of Cicero and asked him to translate a passage. When Psalmanazar had laboriously written it out in his strange script, Innes coolly put it in his pocket and asked him to do it again. Psalmanazar soon got himself into a mess he could not get out of, which was exactly what Innes had counted on. For he had a plan of his own.

In the first place, he said, stop claiming to be a Japanese; too many people know something of that country. But nobody knows Formosa. (Except, possibly, the Dutch—who built a fort there in the seventeenth century and maintained it for thirty-seven years. But they had been expelled forty years before.) Next, he said, let me baptize you into the Anglican Church. Cornered, the young man consented.

Major General Lauder himself stood as godfather, and even gave his name in baptism. Innes wrote immediately to Henry Compton, Bishop of London, of this remarkable conversion, and the Bishop invited them both to come to London.

Baptized George Lauder, the young Formosan (who had in fact never been farther east than the Rhine) went on being known as Psalmanazar—a name he had fashioned from one in the Second Book of Kings. He never told his real one. His arrival in London as the Bishop's protégé raised him at one step from obscurity to the talk of the realm. For Henry Compton was not only Bishop of London but the son of an earl, the man who had performed the coronation ceremony of William and Mary, and a powerful member of the Privy Council.

Entertained by such weighty lords as the Earl of Pembroke, and an honored guest of the Royal Society, Psalmanazar soon had London eating out of his hand. Everyone wanted to catch at least a glimpse of him, or preferably watch as he dined on raw flesh, roots, and herbs. A man from Formosa was as rare as a man from Mars would be today.

The story Psalmanazar told sounded like a tale out of the Arabian Nights. A Jesuit posing as a Japanese had come to his far-off island, he said, had entered his father's house as a Latin tutor (Latin in Formosa!), and had become Psalmanazar's companion and confidant. After four years this Father de Rode, as he called him, wanted to return "home" to Japan and then visit all the Christian countries. Psalmanazar begged to be taken along. The Jesuit, after many refusals, finally gave in, pledging him to secrecy. When Psalmanazar had stolen enough gold from his father to finance their travels, they sneaked away, sailing first to the Philippines and then to Europe, where they ended their long tour

—it lasted almost a year—at a Jesuit monastery in Avignon.

Now the Jesuits tried to convert him, he said: by arguments, by flattery and promises, and then by threats. The young man would not budge. He was threatened with the Inquisition. Alarmed at last, he made his escape by disguising himself and bribing a watchman. Wandering through Germany, he was finally caught by recruiting officers. When he tried to get off by pleading his alien birth, the captain of the guard at Cologne told him: "Though you are a pagan, you may serve in the Army as well as the best Christian."

And that was how a young Formosan had found himself involved in the War of the Spanish Succession.

Psalmanazar fascinated the Londoners not only with his strange diet and his queer language but by his quick wit and aptness in argument. But was he really a Formosan?

From the very beginning there were those who doubted. Yet the public approval of the Bishop of London was a weighty recommendation. When doubters spoke up, they usually took such a beating from the quick-tongued Formosan that others hesitated to tackle him.

Gilbert Burnet, the famous Bishop of Salisbury, asked Psalmanazar for proof that he was Formosan. Avoiding a direct answer, Psalmanazar asked him to suppose he were in Formosa and had to prove he was an Englishman. What would the Formosans say? "You look as like a Dutchman as any that ever traded to Formosa."

To prove his authenticity he translated the catechism into Formosan—or what he claimed to be Formosan. Written from right to left, in such arcane characters as London had

never seen before, it made a great hit. So much so that Psalmanazar felt encouraged to write a *Description of Formosa* which appeared in 1704, complete with engravings of the buildings, costumes, sacrificial altars, vehicles, and other items of Formosan life (see illustrations on these pages).

Formosan fiddlesticks! said Father Fountenay, a Jesuit just returned from China who turned up in London and denounced Psalmanazar as a complete fraud. Formosa, he said, was no part of Japan, as Psalmanazar held it to be, but tributary to China. There was not a word of truth in Psalmanazar's description of the island, and as for the language, it was a pure invention.

Londoners, aroused to a renewed interest in their young visitor, now hotly debated his authenticity. When the Royal Society announced a debate between Psalmanazar and Fountenay on February 2, 1704, the august members turned out in force. Fountenay insisted that Formosa belonged to China, as it then did. Psalmanazar held for Japan.

"By what name do the Chinese call Formosa?" Psalmanazar asked.

"I know no other name for it but Tyowan," said the priest.

Psalmanazar insisted that Tyowan (Taiwan) was a quite different island. "The Chinese call our Island by the name of Pak-Ando, which agrees with Gad-Avia, as we call it, both of which signify the Island Formosa."

"Pak, Pak," said Fountenay, "there is not such a word in the whole Chinese language that ends with a consonant as Pak doth."

Psalmanazar deftly pointed out that most of the cities of

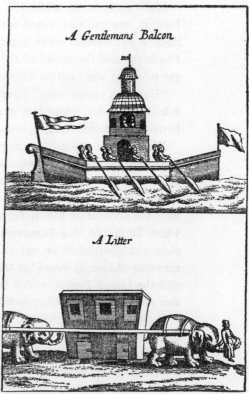

To judge from its pleasure craft and costumes, Formosa had neither high seas nor low temperatures

Human sacrifices were burned on altars

China ended with a consonant—Nanking, Peking, Canton. So when the meeting ended he had the better of it. Fountenay, who apparently realized he had met his match, failed to appear at the home of Lady Powis, and again at Sion College, where he was to have debated with Psalmanazar.

Eight days later, while the argument raged throughout London, the two men dined with the secretary of the Royal Society and several other dignitaries, including the Earl of Pembroke and the envoy of the King of Prussia, who asked the priest to what nation Formosa belonged.

"Here is a young man," Fountenay replied, no doubt with a touch of irony, "who is a native of that country; he can better inform you than I, who have only been in China."

His triumph apparently complete, Psalmanazar now went to Oxford, where he was installed at Christ Church College, again as the guest of the Bishop of London. He spent six months at Oxford studying and lecturing. Crowds came to hear his account of life in Formosa. Among the students to whom he taught "the Formosan language" were some young men who planned to go out as Anglican missionaries. Psalmanazar obligingly provided them with the Apostles' Creed and the Lord's Prayer, which began like this: *"Amy Pornio dan chin Ornio viey, Gnayjorhe sai Lory."*

Psalmanazar's invention of a whole language was the most brilliant triumph of his imposture. He knew Latin and French, and perhaps a few scraps of Dutch and German. But the language he invented shows little resemblance to any of these. It is extremely regular—more so than any real language—with changes of tense indicated by the rise or fall of

the voice, no cases, and three genders. As Psalmanazar himself declared: "I know of no other Language, except that of Japan, that has any great affinity with it; but I find many Words in it, which seem to be deriv'd from several other Languages, only changing either the signification or termination."

It bore, of course, no resemblance at all to Japanese, nor do any of the common words suggest any obvious borrowing: countrymen, *barhaw*; soldiers, *plessios*; man, *banajo*; woman, *bajane*; son, *bot*; daughter, *boti*; father, *pornio*.

Honored as a scholar, Psalmanazar now took steps to increase his reputation.

"I used to light a candle and let it burn the greatest part of the night in my study," he later confessed, "to make my neighbours believe I was plying of my books; and sleeping in my easy chair, left the bed often for a whole week as I found it, to the great surprise of my bedmaker, who could hardly imagine how I could live with so little sleep." He even pretended to have swollen legs from excessive study, and limped as with the gout. At Oxford he did, however, produce a second edition of his *Description of Formosa*, and also left behind him a scholarly study of consular and imperial coins.

Back in London, some of the clergy and other respected gentlemen made up a fund for his maintenance. He floated on a tide of immense popularity, fascinating audiences with tales of human sacrifice, cannibalism, and severe punishments like this: "Whosoever shall strike his King, Intendant or Governor, shall be hang'd up by the Feet till he die, having four Dogs fasten'd to his Body to tear it in pieces."

His book was full of such tidbits. Any Formosan who committed adultery a second time, for instance, was beheaded. But Formosan law gave a man as many wives as he cared to support.

Not only did Formosans eat raw meat, wrote Psalmanazar, but snakes as well. "But before they eat them, they take care to extract all the Poison out of them, which they do after this manner: They take them when they are alive and beat them with Rods until they be very angry; and when they are in this furious passion, all the Venom that was in the body ascends to the Head, which being then cut off, there remains no more Poison in the Body."

We also learn that the Formosans adore their emperor as a god, and how they salute one another (kissing both hands), what each social rank wears, how the poor are cared for. In fact the whole thing sounds far more regular than any known human society. Most remarkable of all was that "They teach the Greek tongue, and every one may learn it in their Academies."

This was more than the Earl of Pembroke (president of the Royal Society), at first a loyal supporter of Psalmanazar, could stomach. Others now began to wonder too. How could he maintain that Formosa was part of Japan? Why was his skin so fair? (He said well-born Formosans lived in underground rooms during the heat of the year.)

The famous astronomer Dr. Edmund Halley innocently inquired how long twilight lasted and how long the sun shone down the chimney every year. Psalmanazar might easily have said he did not remember, he had been so long away from home. But that was not his method. He claimed to remember everything, and he was woefully wrong about the sun in Formosa. Knowing its latitude, Halley easily proved that Psalmanazar's statements about twilight and the sun's declination could not be correct. The word got around. Added to his other errors, it undermined his reputation.

So after nearly five years of triumph he began to slip. Finally a mock advertisement appeared in the *Spectator*:

"On the first of April will be performed at the Play-House in the Haymarket an Opera call'd *The Cruelty of Atreus*.

"N.B. The Scene wherein Thyestes eats his own children, is to be performed by the famous Mr. Psalmanazar, lately arrived from Formosa: the whole supper being set to kettle-drums."

Meanwhile the Scotch chaplain Innes, rewarded for converting the Formosan, had left England as chaplain-general to the English forces in Portugal. With Innes at his elbow, Psalmanazar had had the brass to maintain his huge fiction; but with Innes gone, he grew shaky and finally disappeared for a while from public view.

But who *was* Psalmanazar?

He was merely one of the most successful impostors in history. Born somewhere in the south of France about 1679, he had been educated in several conventual schools, where he was often the top pupil. His easy victories made him so vain and then so eager to be conspicuous that he could not bear to have anyone above him.

At about sixteen he became tutor to two boys, whose mother apparently had hired him with the hope that he would serve her in another capacity. When he did not respond to her advances, she fired him. Penniless, he decided to travel into Germany where his father was living. But how could he get there without money? As a pilgrim, obviously. So he stole a pilgrim's staff and cloak from a chapel, begging as he went and relying on the Latin he had learned from the Jesuits to make his wants known. He found his father at last, but impoverished and unable to help him.

Destitute in a foreign country, the boy recalled what the Jesuits had told him about Japan, where they had preached and converted from 1549 to about 1600 when the government had driven them out. He would pass himself off as a Japanese convert.

The impersonation did him little good. Suspected as a spy, he was thrown into prison. His clothes were now but rags, his body covered with vermin and a repulsive skin disease. Finally, at Liège an enlisting officer took pity on him, fed and clothed him, cured his disease, and put him to work in a coffeehouse he owned at Aix-la-Chapelle, hoping his "Japanese" would attract trade. The customers were not impressed. On his own again, Psalmanazar enlisted in the army of the Elector of Cologne, grew sick, and was mustered out in midwinter with only a "bare loose old frock of blue linen" and shoes so old they soon disintegrated. He enlisted again, and so came to Sluys, where he met Innes.

In some ways the end of Psalmanazar's life was more remarkable than the flamboyant beginning. He sponsored a new kind of paint, called, in his honor, Formosan. It was a failure. Then, after a period which he himself called one of "shameful idleness, vanity, and extravagance," he returned to tutoring. Next he became clerk of a regiment, then a fan-painter, and finally a translator. When a serious illness turned his thoughts toward religion, he read Law's *Serious Call to a Devout and Holy Life* and became a new man.

He also, for his sins, became a free-lance writer, turning out a history of printing and many parts of a big universal history. Always adept at languages, he began to study Hebrew and made himself master of it. Asked to contribute the account of Formosa to a *Complete System of Geography*, he anonymously nailed his own *Description of Formosa* as a fraud and proceeded to describe the country after a Dutch chaplain named Candidius, "though it is to be feared, that upon serious Examination, this will be found to deserve as little Credit, as that of our pretended Formosan."

Working long hours at his desk, Psalmanazar took to opium to sustain himself, raising the dose until he was taking

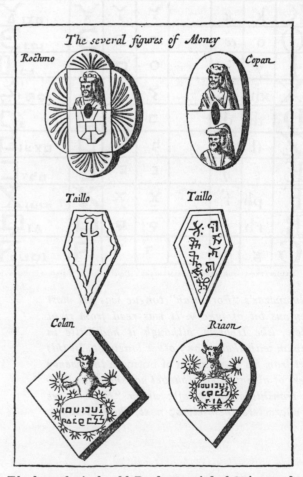

The hypothetical gold Rochmo weighed 8½ pounds

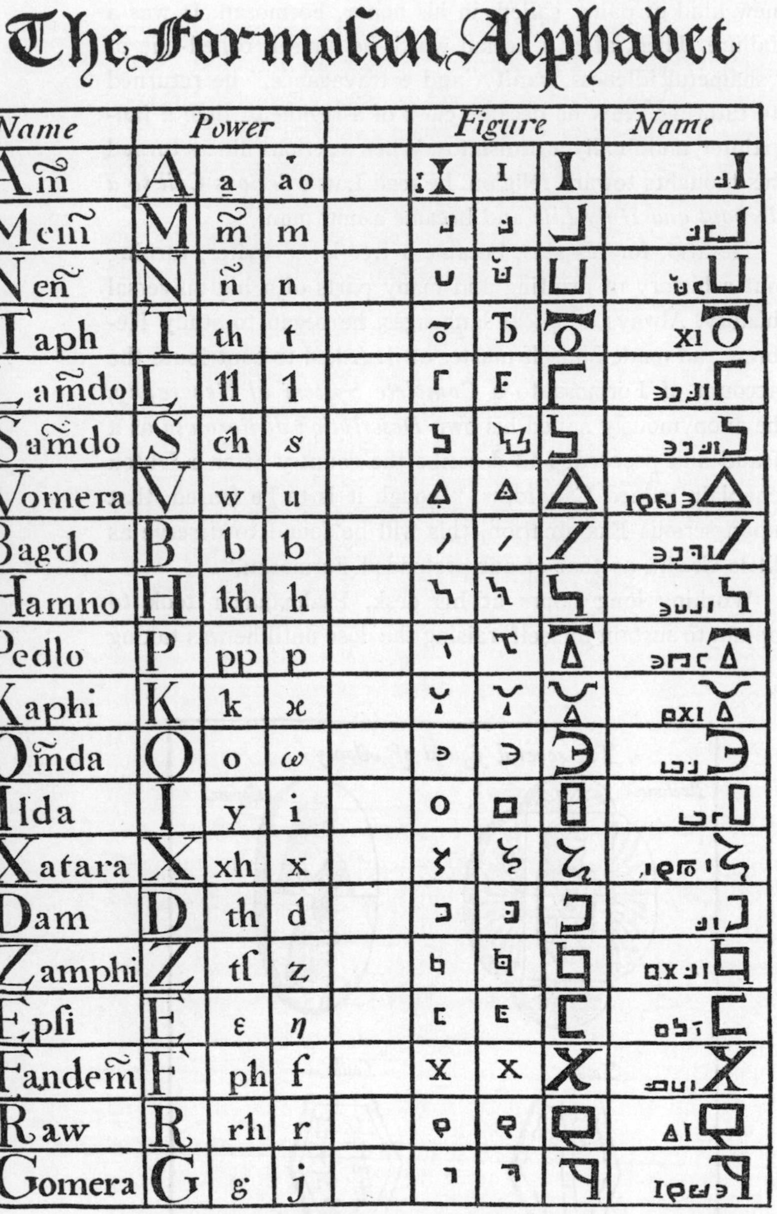

The Formosan Alphabet

Name	Power		Figure			Name
Am	A	a̱	ao	Ⅹ	I	I	⅃I
Men	M	m̃	m	⌐	⌐	⌐	⌐⌐
Nen	N	ñ	n	ʊ	ʊ̆	⊔	⊔
Taph	T	th	t	�	Ђ	⌒	Xı⌒
Lamdo	L	ll	l	Γ	F	⌐	⌐
Samdo	S	ch	s	┗	⍦	┗	┗
Vomera	V	w	u	△	△	△	△
Bagdo	B	b	b	/	/	/	/
Hamno	H	kh	h	٦	٦	٦	٦
Pedlo	P	pp	p	⊤	⊤	△	△
Kaphi	K	k	ж	Y	Y	⋎	⋎
Omda	O	o	ω	∋	Ǝ	Ǝ	Ǝ
Ilda	I	y	i	o	□	日	日
Xatara	X	xh	x	Ɣ	⅗	Ⴑ	Ⴑ
Dam	D	th	d	コ	Ǝ	コ	コ
Zamphi	Z	tʃ	z	ь	ᖯ	ᖯ	ᖯ
Epsi	E	ε	η	Ⴀ	E	┗	┗
Fandem	F	ph	f	X	X	X	X
Raw	R	rh	r	φ	φ	Ω	Ω
Gomera	G	g	j	˥	˥	ʔ	ʔ

ILLUSTRATIONS FROM GEORGE PSALMANAZAR'S *Description of Formosa,* LONDON 1704

Psalmanazar's "Formosan" tongue was his most ingenious bit of fakery. It was read from right to left, like Hebrew, although it had little in common with that or any other language. In this chart from his Description of Formosa *the twenty letters of his invented alphabet are shown in English transliteration at left; under "Figure" are the characters themselves; next, their spellings.*

ten or twelve spoonfuls each night. Even here his vanity would not let him quite alone, for when he decided to lessen the dose, he increased the amount of liquor he mixed with it so that people would still be impressed with his capacity.

Yet Dr. Samuel Johnson, not an easy man to please, when asked who was the best man he had ever known, said: "Psalmanazar. Though a native of France, he possessed more of the English language than any one of the other foreigners who had fallen in my way. George Psalmanazar's piety, penitence, and virtue exceeded almost what we read as wonderful even in the lives of saints."

So Johnson told Mrs. Piozzi. Twenty years after George Psalmanazar had died, in his middle eighties, Johnson told Boswell that the man's piety was so great, "I should as soon think of contradicting a BISHOP."

"I sought after George Psalmanazar the most," he said. "I used to go and sit with him at an alehouse in the city." He added that they belonged to a small club in Old Street— the street where Psalmanazar lived for some years with the curate of Saint Luke's.

That Johnson, knowing of Psalmanazar's imposture, could praise him so extravagantly is proof enough that the "Formosan" must have had a real change of heart. The key to his character seems to be his hunger for praise and attention, rising out of a need generated by his own broken home. Why his father lived in Germany we do not know, but it is clear that the Jesuit teachers whom he worked so hard to please became a sort of substitute father. Pleasing them was an easy matter for him. He had an agile brain, he remembered easily, and this memory won him the praise he hungered for.

Thrown into the world on his own, he naturally used the only strength he had—his memory—to see him through. Stories of Jesuit missionaries in Asia readily came to his mind. The training he had had in Latin made it an easy game for him to invent a language, while the lessons in theology suggested the religious customs which play so important a part in his book.

Even though he was an impostor and a successful one, Psalmanazar's mind was essentially theological. His books drip theology. His Jesuit training had given him a sharp mind for controversy, and when he turned it against them and in favor of Anglicanism, he naturally found a ready welcome in England, where fear and hatred of the Jesuits still sprouted wildly.

The man who gave his imaginary Formosans as many wives as they wanted was never married himself. In his will he desired to be buried like a pauper. Was it humility or a touch of the old stagemanship that made him keep his real name and place of birth forever a secret?

Bradford Smith has written extensively on American history and social institutions, and his articles have appeared in the Saturday Review, AMERICAN HERITAGE, *and other magazines.*

Lifting the Federal Facade

CONTINUED FROM PAGE 27

Henry R. Shepley. They were empowered to act not as mere censors who could check the worst excesses of poor architects, but to represent the department as they might an ambitious private client who, no longer wishing to rely on his own amateur judgment, desired the best possible professional advice. The panel was given responsibility for the selection of architects on a basis of their professional ability alone and for critical supervision of the design process.

The importance of this innovation cannot be overestimated. It meant that for the first time on a routine basis, rather than on the rare occasions when competitions were held, *the design of Federal buildings was completely freed from political pressure.* Although the awarding of Federal commissions is accompanied by an outer show of scrupulous fairness, it is a rare architect of a post office or courthouse who does not have some special entrée in Washington and whose selection depends entirely on professional merit. Since talented architects, on principle and by temperament, are not often found near the pork barrel (Frank Lloyd Wright, for instance, over a seventy-year career never designed a Federal building), mediocrity hitherto has flourished. "When we receive a call from the Hill," conceded an official of the General Services Administration, the agency responsible for most Federal construction, "we jump." When the State Department instituted its program, however, and calls came from the Hill as expected, powerful intercessors were told, "usually to their own great relief," as the *Architectural Forum* put it, "that political favors just aren't part of the ground rules."

The result has been the creation of the finest ensemble of buildings ever sponsored by the United States government. If the embassies and consulates have a style in common, ranging from Harry Weese's airy, richly colored pavilion of wood at Accra to Marcel Breuer's limestone-faced urban block on the Lange Voorhout in The Hague, their similarity resides in an intellectual premise of freedom rather than in any dogmatic attachment to specific forms and materials. Pietro Belluschi defined the unifying philosophy behind these structures when he expressed hope that the architect "will think of style not in its narrower meaning but as a quality to be imparted to the building. . . . His directness and freshness of approach will thus have a distinguishable American flavor."

Directness and freshness of approach; as accurate a phrase as any to sum up the pragmatic vigor of American civilization at its best. The many different approaches possible in any given situation were revealed in the only competition the State Department has conducted, for the London embassy on Grosvenor Square. The site, one of the handsomest in the world, is for that very reason one of the most challenging. To replace a side of historic Grosvenor Square with a Modern building, and not to violate its character, calls for much imagination. Furthermore, in a country such as Eng-

land, where the most advanced structural techniques and industrial materials are available, there could be no thought of attempting literally to duplicate the cut-stone façades of the neighboring old buildings.

The winning design by Eero Saarinen (see page 20), grandly symmetrical, sharing the over-all formality, scale, and horizontal mood of the square, is an extremely powerful concept. To give the wall surfaces an almost baroque vitality, he devised a structural grid of precast Portland stone that will weather to London's traditional black and white. The building is manly, spirited yet reserved, with that hidden fund of poetry which, as Santayana said, exists deep within "every nice Englishman."

At the same time Edward D. Stone was designing an altogether different sort of embassy for New Delhi (page 20). This already celebrated building, which has influenced several other American overseas structures meant for warm climates, stands serenely above its great reflecting pool on a podium of classical dimensions. A projecting roof, borne lightly by golden columns, hovers over the gently glittering little palace. The walls are not true walls, but screens which hold the sun from large glass windows within; and the sun plays about the screens' apertures, emphasizing the repetition of detail that itself seems oriental. Beneath the emblem of the United States one moves through a tall entry into a watery inner court in which fountains spray among tropical plants beneath a lattice which, again, holds off the sun and then allows it to filter downward to the long central pool. The brilliant finish of the building, its almost machined quality of precision, is actually the result of painstaking and exquisite handwork by Indian workers. "This building," the architect has said, "was assembled like the Parthenon."

Will it hold up as truly classical architecture as the Parthenon has: a building so perfect for its own time that it will be for all time? If Nehru has described the embassy as "hauntingly beautiful," some young Indian architects contend that Le Corbusier's great masculine monuments of raw concrete at Chandigarh are closer to ideal public monuments for an emerging nation such as India.

The designers of the new embassies and consulates have shown themselves not only willing but eager to take advantage of the manifold technical resources at their disposal. In hot places, especially—Tangier, Asunción, Karachi, Rabat —they have made inventive use of reinforced concrete, precasting sun screens and parasol roof-shells, with dividends in beauty, utility, and costs.

Sometimes, indeed, the architects seem to be striving too hard for effect, as in John Johansen's proposed circular embassy for Dublin, an ingenious structure inspired by Celtic round towers and built of twisted precast concrete elements, but needlessly complex, it would seem, for so small a building. On the other hand, some structures are deliberately nonpoetic, such as Skidmore, Owings and Merrill's steel-and-glass consulate in Munich, the rationale of which is as strict as the German school of Modern could wish. Between these extremes of understatement and overstatement is a cheerful and quietly elegant building like Minoru Yamasaki's Kobe consulate, set in an ageless garden (page 18).

In spite of the stirring example set by the State Department overseas, however, the Modern is still far from being assimilated in Washington itself. Although the Foreign Buildings Office has received powerful support from the Senate Foreign Relations Committee, a House subcommittee has attacked the overseas building program, taking particular exception to the London embassy and to the proposed design for Dublin (which the FBO thereupon shelved), and threatening to withhold funds in case Eero Saarinen received any further commissions. The State Department itself, housed in a nondescript main building, completed in 1941, in what is called governmental modern (a style that Frederick Gutheim defines as "by, for, and of bureaucrats"), has recently put up a monstrous addition to it in the same style.

The State Department extension is only one of a number of large costly buildings which are being erected as part of a ten-year program scheduled for completion in 1966, which will replace leased and temporary quarters and once more change the official face of Washington. One huge group is to rise on the cleared southwest quadrant, once a good spot from which to photograph the Capitol dome with slums in the foreground. Of this group, rather ominously named Federal Office Buildings 5 through 10A and 10B, Number 9 (pages 22–23) seems from drawings to be the best. Serious architects were engaged for this project, although, as frequently happens, the job was split between two firms, one of which, Hellmuth, Obata & Kassabaum, has consistently done more outstanding work than the other.

Number 9 has been described as a "no-nonsense" building, and it is certainly that. There are no pompous colonnades or other frills, and compared with its nearest architectural neighbors, State and Interior, its design is a distinct relief. It is skillfully organized in double wings, so that the interiors will have a large degree of light and air which older labyrinthine government buildings, with their cramped inner courts, badly lack. A repetitive window pattern, defined by a limestone grid, tactfully blends into the total composition. The building is eminently "safe." But a designer as gifted as Gyo Obata has apparently been held in check, and the verve that even a good plain building should have seems missing. The classical friezes are gone, but the mausoleum effect remains.

The agency responsible for these buildings is the General Services Administration which, acting for the government, is the largest single patron of architecture in the nation. One and a quarter billion dollars of commissions have been awarded by the GSA since the Eisenhower administration ended the Truman lease-purchase policy; one is hard put to find more than a few outstanding designs in the whole lot.

The difference between the results achieved by the foreign building program and those of the GSA can be appreciated by a comparison of the Bangkok embassy by John Carl Warnecke (page 21) and the proposed Federal court and office building in San Francisco (page 23), in whose design Warnecke also participated. The embassy is to be a wide, spacious lake pavilion, white and cool, which lifts on slender concrete uprights from a *klong* in a country permeated with water. In the best sense it is a personal creation as well as a public work of art.

In San Francisco, on the other hand, as might be expected, Warnecke did not work alone on a building that will cost $45,000,000. His firm was teamed with three others, none of which is celebrated for eminence in design. One of the associated architects, for instance, is Albert F. Roller, author of the grandiose Masonic Memorial Temple of white marble, which disfigures Nob Hill with a burst of vulgarity reminiscent of Mussolini's architecture. Considering all, the Federal Building is about the best that could be obtained under the circumstances. It is a doggedly plain tower of concrete and glass, twenty stories high, which will close the northern vista of the Civic Center with a heavy vertical form. The plaza in front is a welcome addition—more Federal buildings should have them. But much more could have been done.

When a fine Federal building appears in this country today, it seems largely an accident. The best chances lie with the special structure, intended either for a unique purpose or an important location, or both, and likely to receive a great deal of attention from the public and Congress. The Modern, when forced to fight, has plenty of defenders; when allowed its full scope and splendor, as in Edward D. Stone's U.S. Pavilion at the recent Brussels Fair, it is likely to win over much of the opposition.

Therefore, even though West Point was endowed only a generation ago with an ensemble of neo-Gothic buildings, the construction two years ago of the Air Force Academy (pages 22–23) in a Modern idiom is perhaps not such "a miracle" as Nathaniel A. Owings of the firm that designed it claims. Whether the Skidmore, Owings and Merrill style was the correct one for the Air Academy is open to question; but the great truss roof of the cadet dining hall, supported only by sixteen columns and covering one and a half acres of unobstructed space, must be accounted one of the chief works of the contemporary movement in America. Surely it can serve, as Yeats said public art should, as a nest for eagles.

Here and there across the country other unusual government structures are doing their part to make this nation, architecturally, more than a nest for sparrows. The Tennessee Valley Authority continues its superior record for functional design in the splendid diagonal lines of the conveyors at the Johnsonville, Tennessee, steam-electric plant. The armed

MARTHA BLAKE

Although Henry Adams scorned it as an "architectural infant asylum," the old State, War and Navy Building was greatly admired in the Washington of the 1880's. Its period-piece originality has won it many partisans today, eager to save it from demolition.

forces often do well, particularly when local officers can act with some independence and engage a man like Ernest J. Kump to design a colorful swimming pool for Coast Guard trainees at Alameda, California (page 24); but this again is largely chance. Of the smaller government agencies, the National Park Service may stand as a model. Because of a fresh interpretation of a thoughtful law of 1916, the Park Service has given up log-cabin design, and commissioned a group of outstanding visitors' centers. Between the stark hills at Dinosaur National Monument in Utah (page 25) the roof of Anshen & Allen's bold structure of steel and concrete flies like an asymmetrical checkmark.

There is no reason why every Federal design cannot be as fundamentally imaginative, if not so overtly dramatic, as Anshen & Allen's. Fine architecture exists first of all in the minds of fine architects, and the government now needs them more urgently than ever. The international struggle now taking place for control of the future will be decided, one might say, by rational control of the environment. Thus when Minoru Yamasaki was asked to design the American exhibit at the World Agricultural Fair, which opened last month at New Delhi, he was forced to consider a number of problems customarily beyond the realm of the architect.

The exhibit (pages 26–27) was not only of profound human importance due to its potential meaning for India, which must improve its agricultural methods drastically or face famine, but it was also of great political significance because the United States would be competing there with the Soviet Union and Communist China. From past experience at Brussels and elsewhere, their approach, both architecturally and

psychologically, was expected to be heavily propagandistic. Yamasaki did not wish to compete on that basis, and he did wish to respect the long tradition of Indian culture, which has produced some of the finest architecture in the world.

As a man familiar with some of the less attractive sides of American life, including racial prejudice, Yamasaki put himself in the place of the Indians and decided that "their belief in democracy could be furthered and their confidence gained by a gentler approach." And so he designed the exhibit as "a series of experiences," as he termed it. First the colonnade of gilded domes (Indian in form but cast in reinforced concrete) comes into sight. Then visitors mount an easy ramp, and suddenly they are walking beneath gay domes on terrazzo platforms that float over an artificial lake filled with fountains and bowls of flowers. Amid color and a spirit of welcome, the Indians pass through indoor and outdoor exhibits, examining cattle, driving tractors, seeing a miniature country fair and a children's section with carousels and a Ferris wheel, and then marketing and processing displays and an open-air theater where square dances are held. Finally, they reach the atomic energy building in which a vision of the future of farming is shown, together with a reactor. And at the end the architect thought it would be good to say farewell graciously in a garden. The building is temporary, but no doubt the experience of it will remain. Yet at home, in rich and great America, experiences like this, which make great architecture, remain all too rare.

Allan Temko has on several occasions written about art and architecture, both contemporary and historical, for HORIZON.

New Life in the Old Opera House

TEXT CONTINUED FROM PAGE 15

Maria Golovin is a blind man of almost equally weak-minded character. The truly heroic and noble hero seems to be outside Menotti's psychological vocabulary. Moreover, his heroines (in *The Saint of Bleecker Street, Maria Golovin,* and the libretto of Samuel Barber's *Vanessa*) are inclined to be rather fluttery females. They are outshone, in spite of Menotti's obvious intentions, by stronger female characters who play lesser roles but who feel more compelling emotions. From the point of view of character, *The Consul,* first performed in 1950, is more satisfying, since it deals with a deeply human and pertinent theme—the despair of displaced individuals in conflict with heartless bureaucracy.

Too often Menotti presents himself as a portrayer of minor, sentimental, visionary, and exotic emotions. But the world owes him a profound debt as the man who first understood and revived the art of opera after its near demise, and he is still young enough to have his finest works ahead of him.

Douglas Moore, whose *Ballad of Baby Doe* was a hit from the time of its New York première three years ago, is a totally different kind of composer. He does not write his own librettos, and he has been fortunate in finding dramatists of unusual talent—Stephen Vincent Benét, John Latouche, Arnold Sundgaard—to collaborate with him. Although he is a musician of vast experience in all forms and styles of composition, he has renounced all the modernistic tricks and devoted himself to pure, uncluttered melody based on the vernacular of American popular and folk music. One does not find, in the score of *The Ballad of Baby Doe,* or in that of its slightly less ambitious predecessor, *The Devil and Daniel Webster,* a single technical affectation or a moment of self-conscious pomposity. The music is direct, accessible even to those who like Broadway musicals, and eloquent as only simple, unadorned lyricism can be. This is not to say that Moore merely writes show tunes. His operas demand singing of high quality, and are woven together with the utmost sophistication. But they are securely rooted in a musical language that any American audience can understand. So far, his masterpiece is *The Ballad of Baby Doe.* It has a strong drama—at once masculine and tender —dealing with the silver boom in the Rocky Mountains at the turn of the century. It presents a story of love, devotion, and renunciation, in which the hero, Horace Tabor, mayor of Leadville, Colorado, his faithful second wife, Baby Doe, and his bitter, abandoned, but still generous, first wife, Augusta, emerge in John Latouche's libretto as absorbing psychological studies. Both its setting and its music recall the Wild West of the cowboy films and the mining camp stories of Bret Harte, but it is basically a powerful theater piece, constructed on lines reminiscent of classical tragedy. It is a truly American opera, and is also perhaps the most effective and engaging work of its kind yet to be produced in this country.

Even before the Ford Foundation inaugurated its festival, Carlisle Floyd, a composer still in his twenties, burst upon the New York opera scene with *Susannah,* a tight little musical drama with origins in American folk song. It was an instant success. *Susannah* is set in the Baptist, hillbilly South, deals with the persecution of an innocent and beautiful heroine by a hypocritical and lust-maddened evangelist who rouses the prudish townsfolk against her, and ends with the shooting of the evangelist by the heroine's brother. All this is heightened by music of the most natural and appropriate sort, evoking the atmosphere of rural life in the Southern countryside in very much the same idiom as is found in its own songs, dances, and revivalist hymns. Technically, there are some crudities about *Susannah.* Its orchestration is a little naïve, and its vocal line does not always show the skill in dealing with vowel and consonant sounds that one expects from a master craftsman. But its libretto (written by the composer himself) is intensely dramatic, and the music has qualities of freshness and inspiration that immediately proclaimed a major talent.

As if to compensate for *Susannah's* musical naïveté, Floyd next embarked on *Wuthering Heights,* a complex romantic opera, full of musical elaboration, and based, of course, on Emily Brontë's novel. On the whole, it proved a less successful venture than *Susannah,* and one should probably regard it as a transitional work reflecting the growing pains of a youthful artist. It is more pretentious, but far less communicative, than the earlier work, and some critics felt that in abandoning the simplicity of his hillbilly, camp-meeting musical vocabulary, Mr. Floyd had entered upon an area of which he was not yet a master. There was one resplendent thing about *Wuthering Heights,* however, and that was its libretto, again written by the composer. This showed him retaining all his genius for the theater, even though the quality of the music never soared to anything approaching true lyricism. Carlisle Floyd is obviously a man to watch. He has great talents, and, if he succeeds in taming his newly found technical vocabulary with an infusion of the sort of melodic inspiration he showed in *Susannah,* he is likely someday to produce a big opera of lasting value.

Vittorio Giannini, like Douglas Moore, is a veteran who has spent a lifetime composing orchestral and other types of music. An American by birth, he has a deep knowledge of the Italian operatic idiom, and his *Taming of the Shrew,* created originally for the NBC Opera and later included in the Ford Foundation's first festival, is to all intents and purposes an Italian *opera buffa* in English. It is perhaps more formal in conception than most of the other operas of the modern American school. It uses the vocal resources of an opera house with practiced skill, providing arias and ensembles for its cast in such a way as to exploit vocal display of the traditional sort, and it involves drama (based on Shakespeare, of course) of really comic character. It is exceedingly well-knit, effective on the stage, and, though it contains few departures from the conventions of the past, it is a model of sound operatic construction, filled with good vocal lines, a deft handling of theatrical situations, and robust orchestration.

The late Kurt Weill, an American by adoption, whose *Threepenny Opera* has remained a classic of musical satire, threw over the mannerisms of German postwar music when he arrived in this country in the early 1930's and devoted himself to writing American musical shows. All of them were conscientiously conceived from the technical standpoint, and several were quite successful on Broadway. At least one of them, *Street Scene* (based on Elmer Rice's play), has the character of a true opera—so much so, in fact, that it was one of his least successful Broadway ventures. It is a tragedy, for one thing, and, for another, its musical texture is more complicated than the Broadway audience usually expects, or gets. A year ago the American Opera Festival decided that *Street Scene* was an opera, and presented it as such with considerable success. Its score is jazzy and reflects the American vernacular. Theatrically it is all one could ask for, and it contains a number of lovely tunes. Considered strictly, it sometimes begs the operatic question by presenting its most gripping moments in spoken dialogue rather than song. Purists may consider it a hybrid work—half musical show, half opera—but it is indubitably a fine contribution to the musical theater.

The surprise of last year's festival was Robert Ward's *He Who Gets Slapped,* based, with some alterations, on Leonid Andreyev's play of the same title. Ward had previously been known as a composer of well-organized and pleasantly lyric symphonies and songs. In this, his first opera, he showed a poetic, delicate, and melodious approach to theatrical music, which heightened the nostalgic and atmospheric qualities of the original play. The opera—a variant on the perennial Pagliacci, or "Laugh, Clown, Laugh" theme—is an affectionate study in backstage circus life. Its remodeled ending is gentler and more poetic than the melodramatic shambles with which Andreyev's play ends. The mysterious clown, who is the hero, enters the drama as a sort of *deus ex machina,* falls in love with the lady bareback rider, renounces his love on finding that she herself is in love with a young aerialist, assists her to consummate her attachment, and in the end, disappears as mysteriously as he came, after some touching philosophical observations on the nature of the human plight.

These men, at the moment, seem to have accomplished most for America's little operatic renaissance, as represented in the productions at the New York City Center. But there are many others whose works entitle them to appreciation. There is, for example, Samuel Barber's *Vanessa*, which achieved the honor of a full-scale production at the Metropolitan Opera House—a work of considerable sophistication,

containing some stunning moments, but one that, especially in its opening act, still reflects the dissonant complexities of what I see as the European decadence. There is Marc Blitzstein's *Regina,* based on Lillian Hellman's *The Little Foxes* —a very well-constructed affair which once enjoyed a moderate Broadway run, but which suffers slightly from the fact that *The Little Foxes* is too shrill and bitter a play to make good operatic material. There is Norman dello Joio's *The Triumph of St. Joan,* a work by an extremely gifted composer, which also suffers a bit from libretto trouble owing to the rather static religious austerity of its subject. There is the late Robert Kurka's *The Good Soldier Schweik,* the work of a very talented man who was somewhat too attached to the grim, satirical idiom of the Weimar Republic to write eloquent opera.

Then, there are some very young men who show distinct promise, but who have not as yet fulfilled their maximum potentialities. Among them are Marc Bucci, whose *Tale for a Deaf Ear* contains some magnificent vocal writing, but which is a little too complex in its metaphysical ramifications to be clear to the average audience as a drama. There is also the very young Lee Hoiby, whose short opera *The Scarf* indicates a promising talent, but one not yet entirely at home in the field of musical theater. Another is Dominick Argento, whose *The Boor,* based on a story by Chekhov, is a very neat little *opera buffa.* Doubtless there are also a considerable number of additional composers whose works have not yet come to this writer's attention.

The element that runs through all of the best of these works is their unpretentiousness, clarity, and dramatic skill. They are primarily light and enjoyable works, unfettered by doctrinaire musicological theories. If the school has not as yet produced a Mozart or a Wagner or even a Puccini, this is hardly cause for alarm. Its work is not, of course, comparable to that of the greatest figures of operatic history. But perhaps this is the place to point out that opera is a very comprehensive and often imperfect art form, and that it has, throughout history, meant different things to different people. Its constants are theater, communicative music, and the expression of emotion by means of song. The Germans and Austrians, and that great Italian master Giuseppe Verdi, built it into a magnificent combination of symphonic music and psychologically complicated drama, producing some of the greatest art works of all time in the medium. The Americans are, at present, feeling their way toward an easily understandable combination of drama and song. At least they are composing operas by the hundreds, and audiences are finding some of them moving and pleasing. Perhaps, out of the new tradition they are evolving, a few real masterpieces will someday emerge. At any rate, the groundwork for them is being laid.

As critic for The New Yorker, *Winthrop Sargeant comments regularly on the world of music, which knew him first as a violinist. He has also written widely of the other arts.*

The Dream of the South Seas

TEXT CONTINUED FROM PAGE 31

man Melville. And even Melville, at the time of his going, in 1842, was not yet a writer but simply a young and restless man off to sea in the ancient tradition. That he came home a writer, however, is a matter of history. And of him, more than of any author, it may be said that milieu created artist no less than artist created milieu. A deck hand on a Yankee whaler, he jumped ship—also in the old tradition—in the Marquesas Islands, moved on to Tahiti and Hawaii, and from experience and imagination wove tales that were to hold the world spellbound.

Today it is *Moby Dick,* and that alone, that gives him his place in the first rank of our writers. But in his own time the white whale and mad Ahab, its pursuer, aroused far less interest than the brown warriors and lissome maidens of *Typee* and *Omoo,* who fitted perfectly into the fabric of the burgeoning South Seas Dream. Indeed, Melville's Fayaway, the seductive nature sprite of Typee Valley, may safely be said to have set the style for island heroines for generations to come. And the traditional identification of the South Seas with literary "escape" received added impulse from his actual escape from his whaler.

After Melville came, if not the deluge, a steady stream of articulate travelers. For by the mid-nineteenth century, it had become possible to visit the Pacific without necessarily being a member of a ship's crew or an expedition; and writers are notoriously creatures who prefer to be on their own. Some merely came and saw and departed. Others came and stayed. Some ranged widely, and others confined themselves to limited areas. They were of many nationalities—with British, French, and American predominating—and among them were as many disparate temperaments and points of view as there were individuals. Only two things may, self-evidently, be said of the lot of them. All were what one might call "centrifugal" rather than "centripetal": men whose sights were on horizons rather than on roots and homeland. And all, in one way or another, had come under the spell of the South Seas Dream.

Man, in his time, has come under many spells; and it seems to me that among those involving far places, this particular one requires the least exegesis. Why men climb mountains can (as I know rather well) be a poser. Why they are lured to freezing arctic, burning desert, sodden jungle, or inky sea bottom may be all but incomprehensible to the less adventurous.* But the South Seas Dream, as heretofore noted, is in the public domain; its symbols are alluring to almost all, and there are few who would ask the island voyager, "Why did you go there?" Why he stayed there or left there, why he loved or loathed it, why he prospered or foundered, are, to be sure, different matters. And the answers can be found only in each individual mind and spirit.

Take two who came and stayed—the two greatest: Robert Louis Stevenson and Paul Gauguin. Sailing from San Francisco in 1888, Stevenson went to the islands not only as a writer and traveler, but as a chronic invalid wracked by tuberculosis; and there he found happiness and a measure of health before death took him six years later. At the time of his setting out he was already famous. He voyaged with his family, mostly in privately chartered boats. In Western Samoa, where he finally settled, he was the island celebrity, and his home, *Vailima,* became a Pacific landmark. As a writer, he was there as elsewhere a sentient and accomplished artist, and better island literature than his *In the South Seas* and *A Footnote to History* has yet to be written. But in his life—with due allowance for geographical transplantation—he remained essentially what he had been before: a cultured and distinguished late Victorian gentleman.

Today, in our (for good reason) unromantic age, R.L.S.'s star is at least in semi-eclipse. In reverse, Gauguin, a mid-twentieth-century giant, was in his own time nobody. Or even, by French bourgeois standards, worse than nobody, for he had once been a supposedly respectable businessman who abandoned wife, home, and conventional decency for the life of an outcast. There were no half-measures in his nature. When he went out to Tahiti for the second time, in 1895, he made the self-casting-out complete, in what is unquestionably the most bitter and total renunciation of the civilized world that a man of genius has ever made. Happiness? One doubts if he knew what happiness was—or cared. Health? His only interest in that seemed to be to wreck it as thoroughly as possible. By the time he died in the Marquesas, in 1903, he was a squalid ruin of a man—and the creator of immortal paintings. And in South Seas annals he remains today the single authentic specimen (for there have been counterfeits aplenty) of the to-hell-with-it beachcomber genius.

As against such occasional stayers, there have of course been many birds of passage. One of the earliest was Mark Twain, who in 1866, while still young and comparatively un-

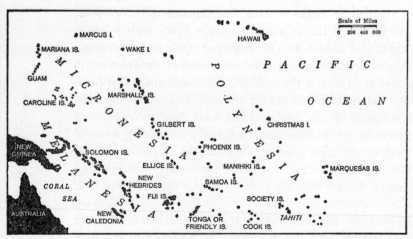

Scores of archipelagoes still harbor the South Seas Dream

*See the article "Why Men Seek Adventure" by Wilfrid Noyce in HORIZON for September, 1958.

known, visited Hawaii as correspondent for a California newspaper. He went no farther however, and his true interests lay elsewhere. Only by geographical courtesy can he be called an associate member of the South Seas fraternity.

The same is true of another, and slightly later, first-magnitude writer; to wit, Joseph Conrad. But with notable differences, for Conrad was, in bones, blood, and long experience, a man of the sea, and no one, before or since, has spun the dream of far places more cogently or authentically. His province, however, was not the true South Seas of Mela-Micro-Polynesia, but rather the larger subcontinental islands of the East Indies. And it was on the Indian, not the Pacific Ocean that his greatest sea stories unfolded.

Of writers in languages other than English, perhaps the most influential, in the late nineteenth century, was Pierre Loti, who sailed the Pacific as a junior officer in the French Navy. A romantic if there ever was one, he created, in *Le Mariage de Loti,* an image of Tahiti that fitted perfectly into the fabric of the South Seas Dream. And his semifictional heroine, Rarahu—gentle, lovely, and doomed—ranks with Melville's Fayaway as an archetype, if not of what an island enchantress actually is, at least of what Western imagination *wants* her to be.

If contrast is again in order, one has but to turn to our own Henry Adams, who toured the islands in 1890–91. Here is the almost complete antithesis of the romantic escapist; and the imagination boggles at the notion of his settling permanently in the Pacific, à la Stevenson or Gauguin. Wealthy and fastidious, the very model of an intellectual Boston Brahmin, he traveled to this part of the world, as he traveled elsewhere, to broaden his horizons—and then return to his proper milieu near the seats of the mighty. Yet even he felt the fascination of what, in Samoa, he called "the kingdom of old-gold," and he set down his impressions more vividly and accurately than many a bemused romancer. With him in his travels was his friend, the artist John La Farge, whose paintings, often highly idealized, contributed their share to the South Seas Legend. But to him, as to Adams, paradise was not *only* for legends. It was part of the living, changing pattern of the larger world from which he came. And in his *Reminiscences,* echoing the spirit of the new American imperialism, he wrote: "The Pacific should be ours, and it must be."

Such as these were the VIP tourists, for whom the South Seas were merely an interlude in busy, far-ranging lives. Others, less well known, spent long years there, and in point of personal experience, knew them far better. One of the earliest was Charles Warren Stoddard, Californian contemporary of Mark Twain, Bret Harte, and Ambrose Bierce, who made many trips through the islands, contributing stories and sketches to popular magazines. Another was Lloyd Osbourne, stepson and sometime collaborator of Stevenson, who, as a young man, came with R.L.S. to Samoa, stayed on for several years after the latter's death, and often broke tradition by writing of the islands not with rapture but with humor. A

Paul Gauguin was a great print maker as well as painter. Such woodcuts as his Tahitian Carrying Bananas, *done after 1895, brought about a revival and revolution of the art.*

third—and the most experienced of all—was the Australian Louis Becke, a trader, prospector, and wandering adventurer who was at best a semiprofessional as a writer, but whose quarter of a century on the scene provided him with a fabulous store of firsthand material.

From the turn of the century to the First World War the stream was at full tide. And here, as before, the pilgrims were widely various both as men and writers. Rebellious and truculent, the Angry Young Man par excellence of his day (and paradoxically a socialist awash in racial prejudice), Jack London cruised the Pacific for two years and wrote the full-bodied action stories and sketches of *South Sea Tales* and *The Cruise of the Snark.* From England came Rupert Brooke, the golden boy of his literary generation, to write the tender lyrics of "Waikiki" and "Tiare Tahiti." And along, too, of course, came the young Somerset Maugham, with sardonic eye and urbane pen, to create a whole gallery of interlopers in Eden, including a lady called Miss Sadie Thompson. London and Brooke each made his one tour and died soon thereafter. Most of Maugham's long life has been spent in the antipodal world of Mayfair and the French Riviera, but the South Seas Dream has never wholly faded from his memory.

In the early 1900's the phrase "mass media" was happily still uninvented. But this was nevertheless the period in which the South Seas Dream became, for good and all, a standard marketable product. H. de Vere Stacpoole's *The Blue Lagoon,* Robert Keable's *Tahiti: Isle of Dreams,* and Frederick O'Brien's *White Shadows in the South Seas* led a procession of thumping best sellers that introduced palm and lagoon, grass skirt and brown maiden to a host of new easy-does-it readers. Richard Walton Tully's *A Bird of Paradise* brought to the stage, with enormous success, a lavish omnibus pageant of old Hawaii. And from these and similar sources came the ultimate in dream merchandising, the films of Hollywood, in which reality vanished into Never-Never land, with gross receipts as Magna Carta and Dorothy Lamour as fairy queen.

At this extreme, of course, we are off in a far different world, both of contour and motivation, from that in which we

125

Gauguin's woodcut Maruru *shows Tahitians before an idol*

started. The isles of desire have become strictly the $outh $eas. But at least it is *only* an extreme; for even with wholesale commercialization and a booming sellers' market, there have been those who have clung to the old untarnished dream. James Norman Hall and Charles Nordhoff, best known of island writers in the years following World War I, were, to be sure, enormously successful with their *Bounty* trilogy and other books. But money could scarcely have been the prime interest of men who made the South Pacific their permanent home, took Polynesian wives, raised island families, and became a part of the new world of their adoption. Indeed, in their lives and work, Nordhoff and Hall present the best examples of men of the West who dreamt the South Seas Dream, followed it, cherished it, and made it fruitful and happy.

For others, who felt the call no less strongly, the story was far different. Surely no one has committed his life to the islands more wholly than Robert Dean Frisbie, who, like Nordhoff and Hall, went out to them in his youth and remained to the end, living often on tiny and remote atolls with no fellow Westerner within hundreds of miles. Frisbie, however, won no great success in writing, and it is open to doubt if he found happiness in his isolation. Like Gauguin's his renunciation was complete. He followed the exile's path. And if he found a freedom rare indeed in the modern world, he paid for it in loneliness, drunkenness, sickness, and early death.

Even more of a loner (for Frisbie had a wife and children) was the Frenchman Alain Gerbault, a solitary round-the-world sailor, who loved the tropic islands with a somber passion, and wrote broodingly of the crimes that civilization had wrought upon them. He too was not a finder—nor, one feels, even a seeker—of happiness, for his dream was an obsession with a world that was irrevocably gone.

Except for Germany's loss of her colonies, the First World War had small direct effect upon the South Pacific. That of the Second was, of course, incalculable. Ships and planes, arms, machines and material—the whole paraphernalia of modern war and modern living—was poured into, and across, the islands; with them came men by the hundreds of thousands, and if only one certainty emerged from it all, it was that the face of the South Seas was changed forever. Inevitably, a vast amount of writing came out of the war; but most of it was *about* the war, with the island world itself merely as stage setting. And most of the writers, at war's end, withdrew from the Pacific with the fleets and armies and turned their attention to other fields. They were observers and reporters of history; not dreamers of the South Seas Dream.

A partial but notable exception was James Michener, whose *Tales of the South Pacific*, both as book and stage musical, is a contemporary classic, and whose fictional Bali-ha'i, conceived in wartime, has become the island equivalent of Eldorado and Shangri-La. Michener was—and is—fascinated by the Pacific for its own sake. He has traveled widely in it since the war, written many more books about it, and now makes his home in Hawaii. But he is a man of his time. Our time. And his Bali-ha'i is but a fleeting phantom. His abiding vision of the South Seas is not an escapist's dream, but a factual picture of a part of the modern world, beset on all sides by that world's problems and realities.

Such has been the case, too, with most other postwar Pacific chroniclers. For here is no longer a Never-Never land, shrouded in remoteness and mystery. It is there, plain for all to see; and when a thing is *there*, it is no longer fancy but fact. As a result, the bulk of recent writing about the area has been nonfictional, ranging from straight reportage through accounts of personal experience, to detailed and carefully researched analyses of island life and culture. In this last category, the outstanding work designed for the general reader is J. C. Furnas's *Anatomy of Paradise,* which, taking the whole Pacific as its domain, debunks the more meretricious aspects of the South Seas Legend with thoroughness and gusto. And in more specialized fields there has been a steady stream of works by anthropologists, sociologists, and indeed every brand of -ologist in the catalogue. As one latter-day voyager, himself a member of the fraternity, recently put it to me: "There's hardly a sandspit or taro patch left in the ocean that hasn't been staked out by a Ph.D."

Knowledge is all to the good. Truth is all to the good. But what, if anything, do they leave of the South Seas Dream? Is it now merely another casualty, another burst bubble, in a world hard put for dreams to cling to? As I stand on my postwar, post-Ph.D., Pacific Island in the year 1959—the Johnny-come-lately with his escort of ghosts—might I just as well, for all that is alluring and magical, be standing at the corner of Fifth and Main, in Middletown, U.S.A.?

I look to the right and see an island village. In the village are mud, rats, roaches, broken bottles, an overturned jeep, a rust-eaten bulldozer, a huddle of tin-roofed shacks, and in the doorway of a shack, a little girl with running eye sores and an old man with elephantiasis. . . . I look to the left and see the tall towers of a radio transmitter. Beyond them is a nest of radar screens and missile-tracking devices; beyond these, in turn, a neat town of prefab houses, with electrical appliances in white kitchens and two-tone hardtops on the driveways. Not far down the concrete road is the lot that has just been purchased for a resort hotel, and across from it, the airport, at which a Stratocruiser—soon to be a jet—is just arriving from San Francisco. Or is it Tokyo? Or Sydney?

These are facts. They are *there*. No wishful thinking can make them go away.

But what of what lies neither right nor left, but straight ahead? For as I look ahead—and now the ghosts draw closer —I see still a different scene, and the rest is gone and forgotten. I see the old clichés, with the old tired names; palm, pandanus, breadfruit, a beach, a lagoon, a white-maned reef. I hear the boom of the surf, feel the breath of the trade wind, watch a canoe with slanted sail move out across the lagoon into the setting sun. And then the sun is down. In its place is dusk, then night, with moon and stars, and on the reef the glinting torches of fishermen. There is the sound of singing voices, the scent of unseen blossoms. . . . And there are no longer tired old words, or limp clichés, but only wonder and beauty; beauty so fresh and pure and authentic that it catches at the throat and heart. And this—yes, this too—is *fact*, no less than the rest. The cliché is fact. The dream is fact.

For the Pacific is broad enough, its myriad islands various enough, to comprise facts beyond number and still leave room for dreams. For the facts contradict each other at every turn. There are the canneries and dockyards and pink hotels of Hawaii, but there are also the fire pits of its great and lonely volcanoes. Wake Island is a mid-ocean filling station on one of the world's major plane routes, but also the immemorial nesting place of a million sea birds. In Fiji there is racial ferment and primeval jungle. In the Marshalls there is a testing ground for modern man's most deadly weapons, and there are lagoons which have yet to float a craft bigger than an outrigger canoe. Tahiti is the island of honky-tonks, drunks, wastrels, poseurs, and beachcombers, but at the same time, no less than in Darwin's day, the "classical" tropical Eden of imagination and desire.

There is magic in its very name: in names like Bora Bora, Moorea, Rarotonga, Mangareva, Abemama, Pago Pago,

In his Te Arii Vahine *Gauguin portrays an island queen*

Noa Noa (Fragrance) *presents an idyllic scene on boxwood.*

Nuku Hiva, Kapingamarangi. Nature, in its works, and the island languages, in their nomenclature, have created symbols for eye and ear almost irresistible to the Western imagination. And added to these, if one searches, if one deviates from the paths of planes and liners, is a way of life—ancient, gracious, and abiding—that even our twentieth century, in its massive onslaught, has been unable wholly to destroy.

Now, at my destination, in the islands at last, I look back across the miles toward the beginning of my journey. And I think of the words of an English writer, Frederic Harrison, which—with what I hope is pardonable presumption—I have long since made my own. "Our present world," he wrote, "is a world of remarkable civilization, but it is not very natural and not very happy. We need, yet, some snatches of the life of youth, to be for a season simply happy and simply healthy. We need to draw sometimes great draughts of simplicity and beauty. We need sometimes that poetry should not be droned into our ears, but flashed into our senses. And man, with all his knowledge and his pride, needs sometimes to know nothing and to feel nothing, but that he is a marvellous atom in a marvellous world." These lines were written a good many years ago; but they seem to me to ring even truer today, in our age of doubts and anxiety, confusion and fear. They were not written with the South Seas specifically in mind; but I can think of no place on earth better able to fulfill such needs of man's spirit. The island is tiny. The sea around it is immense. The perspective is true. Here it is not merely in word or dream, but in overwhelming reality, that man is "a marvellous atom in a marvellous world."

Having first succumbed to the lure of high mountains and produced such famed works on that subject as The White Tower, *the novelist and traveler James Ramsey Ullman now writes from amid the opposite spell of far Pacific islands.*

The Pleasures of the Bastille

CONTINUED FROM PAGE 88

Of course, it was not always easy to tell when a prisoner was genuinely eccentric and when he was feigning. The case of the roommates Danry and Allègre was particularly puzzling, for both were genuinely eccentric and feigning at the same time. They also were the only prisoners who succeeded in preparing a startling surprise for their jailers.

For twenty-six months, beginning in December, 1753, Danry and Allègre, until then the most obstreperous of prisoners, perplexed the authorities by their peaceful behavior. As far as could be ascertained, their time was spent in studies: Allègre, who during his career as a schoolteacher had never had a pupil quite so captive as his roommate, was teaching Danry mathematics, mechanics, and engineering. But there were certain puzzling features in their conduct. Both spent their entire time, for two years, wearing only their dressing gowns; Danry, despite his hoard of shirts, was never seen to wear one; the room, moreover, was underheated, although the firewood supplied in ample quantities was always used up; and their bed and table linen was, for some mysterious reason, chronically ragged. Repeated searches of the room revealed nothing except meticulous tidiness.

On February 26, 1756, early risers who happened to be passing by the Bastille discovered an exhilarating sight. From the platform of one of the towers there floated, attached to a piece of artillery, a rope ladder 180 feet long, shining snow-white, with 188 wooden rungs, each carefully muffled with rags. From a wheelless pulley, attached to the same cannon, there hung a stout rope also gleaming white, 360 feet long. The wall, 4½ feet thick, that separated the moat from the outside world, had been pierced. A few crude tools were found nearby, as well as a wooden ladder with twenty rungs, consisting of several sections carefully fitted together by means of pegs and holes. Outside the wall lay a large leather portmanteau and two suits of soaked and grimy clothes.

Allègre and his pupil had indeed made excellent use of their linen and firewood. They had worked at making ropes and ladders for two years, and had concealed them under some floor boards whenever anyone entered the room. They had removed the bars blocking the flue of their fireplace; had climbed through the chimney to the roof; then hauled up the portmanteau, the rope ladder, the wooden ladder, and a number of tools; let down their paraphernalia; and finally climbed down the rope ladder. They had not forgotten to leave behind a polite note to their good tyrants: "We have caused no damage whatever to any of the furniture of His Lordship the Governor. We have used only strips of blanket that were no longer serviceable; the others are intact. If a few napkins are missing, they can be found beyond the water, in the large moat, where we took them to wipe our feet."

It is with regret that one must report the end of this adventure. Danry was discovered some weeks later in Amsterdam by a French police lieutenant disguised as an Armenian merchant; the Dutch government extradited him to France. Allègre, who was captured in Brussels, ended up in an insane asylum. Danry, after thirty-five years of imprisonment in various places, made a living, until his death in 1805, by selling his memoirs, which became increasingly fanciful in successive editions. He is remembered as Henri Masers de Latude, a name he fabricated sometime during his imprisonment. Much of the legend of the Bastille is the result of his fertile imagination.

"God bless these good tyrants!" Never was tyranny exercised by more gentle and considerate hands than in France just before the Revolution. Only two objections could be made to their debonair methods: first, that one was locked up in the Bastille without a trial, and second, that one could not tell how long one's stay there would be. But to reform this abuse it was not necessary to storm the fortress: a stroke of the pen would have sufficed, and in fact the system was about to be abolished when the Bastille was attacked. Four years after that bastion of despotic arbitrariness had been razed, the revolutionary government passed the Law of Suspects, by which any person, upon simple denunciation, could be arrested, tried (without benefit of counsel), and guillotined, all this in the space of a few hours, to safeguard the newly won freedom of the nation.

J. Christopher Herold is editor-in-chief of the Stanford University Press and author of Mistress to an Age, *the biography of Madame de Staël which won the National Book Award.*

STATEMENT REQUIRED BY THE ACT OF AUGUST 24, 1912, AS AMENDED BY THE ACTS OF MARCH 3, 1933, AND JULY 2, 1946 (Title 39, United States Code, Section 233) SHOWING THE OWNERSHIP, MANAGEMENT, AND CIRCULATION OF HORIZON, published bi-monthly at New York, N. Y. for October 1, 1959.

1. The names and addresses of the publisher, editor, and managing editor are: Publisher, James Parton, Editor, Joseph J. Thorndike, Jr., Managing Editor, William Harlan Hale, all of 551 Fifth Avenue, New York 17, N. Y.

2. The owners are: American Horizon, Inc., 551 Fifth Avenue, New York 17, N. Y.; stockholders owning or holding 1 per cent or more of total amount of stock: American Heritage Publishing Co., Inc.; William Harlan Hale; Oliver O. Jensen; Joseph J. Thorndike, Jr., individually and as Trustee under Declaration of Trust for John Thorndike, dated 12/27/57, as Trustee under Declaration of Trust for Alan Thorndike, dated 12/27/57 and as Voting Trustee under Agreement, dated 2/6/59, for James Parton and Alexander Hehmeyer; all of 551 Fifth Avenue, New York 17, N. Y.

3. The known bondholders, mortgagees, and other security holders owning or holding 1 per cent or more of total amount of bonds, mortgages, or other securities are: None.

4. Paragraphs 2 and 3 include, in cases where the stockholder or security holder appears upon the books of the company as trustee or in any other fiduciary relation, the name of the person or corporation for whom such trustee is acting; also the statements in the two paragraphs show the affiant's knowledge and belief as to the circumstances and conditions under which stockholders and security holders who do not appear upon the books of the company as trustees, hold stock and securities in a capacity other than that of a bona fide owner.

Signed, James Parton, Publisher.
Sworn to and subscribed before me this 20 day of August, 1959. [Seal] Nathan Greenberg, Notary Public (my commission expires March 30, 1960)

The
Natural History
of the
Mermaid

*The siren is clearly immortal, even though a
century has passed since anybody has seen one*

A fifth-century mermaid enlivens the church of San Giovanni Evangelista, Ravenna

By RICHARD CARRINGTON

Babylonian clay seals show fish deities

Mermaid seen on a 16th-century emblem

Homeric sirens exert their fatal allure

The mermaid is perhaps the most glamourous and poetic figure in the whole history of mythology and folklore. To study her natural history may therefore seem a little unchivalrous, and I do not propose to treat it with the scientific precision appropriate to, say, jellyfish or hake. My method will be simply to trace some of the influences, natural, psychological, and spiritual, that have given the mermaid her unique place in the imaginations of men.

First, let us see how she has manifested herself on various occasions to human eyes. Working backwards from our own times, we find that there has been a distressing lack of mermaid sightings during the whole of the present century. This can possibly be put down to the increasing gravity of scientists, who have become dispirited under the vast accumulations of facts that press each year more heavily upon their minds; it may also be due to the amenities of modern ports, which have largely distracted mariners from their traditional occupation of conjuring glamourous visions from the depths of the sea. But in the nineteenth century a less prosaic spirit was abroad, as is shown by the following letter written to *The Times* in 1809 by a Mr. William Munro, a schoolmaster of Thurso in Scotland. It was headed, "The Mermaid Seen on the Coast of Caithness."

Dear Sir—About twelve years ago, when I was a Parochial Schoolmaster at Reay, in the course of my walking on the shore of Sandside Bay, being a warm fine day in summer, I was induced to extend my walk towards Sandside Head, when my attention was arrested by the appearance of a figure resembling an unclothed human female, sitting upon a rock. . . . The forehead was round, the face plump, the cheeks ruddy, the eyes blue, the mouth and lips of a natural form . . . the breasts and abdomen, the arms and fingers of the size of a full grown body of the human species. It remained on the rock three or four minutes after I observed it, and was exercised during that period in combing its hair, which was long and thick, and of which it appeared proud, and then dropped into the sea, from which it did not reappear to me.

(Signed) WM. MUNRO

This was one of many nineteenth-century mermaid reports, some of which aroused widespread interest right up to the end of Queen Victoria's reign. The imaginations of our grandparents were, in fact, particularly mermaid-prone, for the concept of these mysterious maidens of the sea was in tune with the exaggerated romanticism of the time. Prints of mermaids were acceptable on the walls of even the staidest Victorian homes—probably because the presence of scales below the waist conveniently camouflaged any suggestion of the more basic attributes of sex. Such artists as Arnold Böcklin amassed vast fortunes with portraits of wild-eyed sirens tossed among the waves of tempestuous seas (see illustration, page 132), while even such respectable poets as Tennyson occasionally permitted himself to indulge in images of

Sweet faces, rounded arms, and bosoms prest
To little harps of gold.

On a somewhat lower plane, sentimental siren songs, such as Arthur Lloyd's "Married to a Mermaid," were a feature of every music hall in the eighties.

Pressing back farther into time, physical observations of alleged mermaids become increasingly common. The eighteenth century, usually thought of as an age of scepticism and good sense, produced a particularly good crop. Several eighteenth-century mermaids apparently lived off British coasts, while others were seen in regions as far apart as the Arctic and the East Indies.

A Dutch colonial chaplain named François Valentijn reproduced in his *Natural History of Amboina* (1726) a delightful picture of an East Indian mermaid with other queer fish of the region (page 135). From the caption we learn that the mermaid was fifty-nine inches long, lived after being caught for four days and seven hours in a barrel filled with water, and "uttered little cries like those of a mouse." In spite of these vocal limitations, its figure, at least the upper part, had such obvious attractions that King George III was graciously pleased to accept the original picture, and Peter the Great of Russia wrote to Valentijn for further details. These unfortunately the Dutchman was unable to provide, but he intrigued the Czar with an account of another episode in which a mermaid and a merman "of a greenish grey color" were seen swimming together by more than fifty persons. "Should the stubborn world hesitate to believe it," he adds, "it matters nothing, for there are people who would deny the existence of Rome, Constantino-

130

ple, or Cairo, simply because they themselves have not happened to see them."

Although the testimony of schoolmasters and chaplains is obviously of the highest value, an even more impressive account comes from the rugged old seventeenth-century navigator Henry Hudson. The incident occurred off Nova Zembla during one of Hudson's daring attempts to force the Northwest Passage. He describes his mermaid with the same *sang-froid* as you and I might report the sighting of a porpoise:

This evening [June 15] one of our company, looking overboard, saw a mermaid, and, calling up some of the company to see her, one more of the crew came up, and by that time she was come close to the ship's side, looking earnestly on the men. A little after a sea came and overturned her. From the navel upward, her back and breasts were like a woman's, as they say that saw her; her body as big as one of us, her skin very white, and long hair hanging down behind, of colour black. In her going down they saw her tail, which was like the tail of a porpoise, speckled like a mackerel.

References to mermaids occur in medieval and Renaissance natural histories and collections of travelers' tales, but these almost always seem to be based on hearsay rather than direct observation. Most of them can safely be regarded as springing from a fevered imagination, an elaborate flight of alcoholic fantasy, misinterpretation of inadequate facts, and in some cases straightforward honest-to-God lying. To take an example, there is the tale of seven mermen and mermaids captured at Manaar in 1560, and carried to Goa, where they were dissected by Demas Bosquez, physician to the Viceroy, and "their internal structure found to be in all respects conformable to the human." Another account speaks of a merman seen off the coast of Martinique which was approached so closely by several persons that it was seen to wipe its hands across its face and even heard to blow its nose.

Setting such pleasing concepts aside, is it possible to trace any logical pattern in the mermaid legend and to account for its wide distribution and long persistence in human tradition? To answer this question we must turn to the evolution of primitive religion and the history of classical myth and legend, and then to the accounts given by modern science of animals of mermaidlike form.

Our primitive ancestors, we now know, did not recognize one god, as do the majority of Western religions today, but worshiped a number of different objects, persons, and natural forces, each in a different form. Thus there was a separate god for the sun, the moon, and the stars; gods for the rivers, mountains, and lakes; and gods associated with man-made objects such as household goods, weapons, and even agricultural implements. The most important gods were those associated with the more powerful and dramatic natural forces. Hence the great power ascribed by our ancestors to the sun-god, who supplied light and warmth to the world, and to the rain-god, who brought fertility to the parched earth after drought.

One of the most awe-inspiring natural phenomena, to our ancestors as to ourselves, was the sea, and numerous gods and goddesses were associated with it at different times in different regions. Some of these deities were likewise associated with the legend of the Flood—a legend which occurs not only in the Old Testament, but in modified form in many ancient religions and even in the mythologies of primitive peoples today. It is among these water deities of the sea and the Flood that we must seek for the origin of the mermaid legend.

The progenitor of all the glamourous mermaids of later times was in all probability not a woman but a man; yet not quite a man, but a fish deity who came up from the Persian Gulf and landed on the shores of Babylonia to teach the inhabitants of that land the values of civilization. The authority for this story is a priest and astronomer of Babylon known as Berosus, who recorded it in his *History of Syria,* written about 260 B.C. The fish-god was mainly worshiped at Erech, "the place of the ark," where he was known as Oannes. Elsewhere he was known as Oes, Hoa, Ea, Ana, Aun, and Oan, and was sometimes identified with the Biblical Noah himself. He was usually represented as a typical merman, with the bearded head and torso of a man, and a scaly tail below the waist (page 130). But some pictures show him as a normal man with a fish's head worn as a cap, the skin hanging down his back in the form of a cloak. Another Babylonian god, Dagon, is likewise sometimes represented in this double form. Scholars still remain cautious about regarding Dagon as a sea-god, but the poet Milton had no such reservations:

TEXT CONTINUED ON PAGE 134

A mermaid abandons her mortal husband

Bishop Berkeley's coat of arms, Bristol

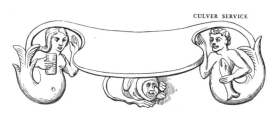

Mermaid miserere, Winchester Cathedral

Merfamily serenade in Lyons Cathedral

131

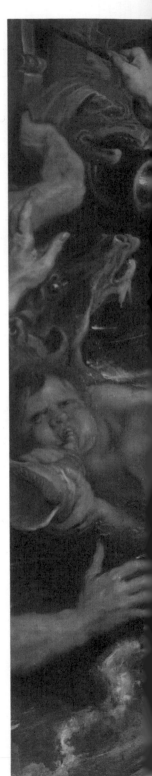

When a friend asked him to design a chandelier, Albrecht Dürer drew this not very functional (only one candle) arrangement of antlers, vine, and beguiling mermaid.

Mermaids, tritons, a seagoing centaur, and a lone female unequipped with fins splash across Arnold Böcklin's watery Sport of the Waves, a sometime German favorite.

The Mermaid in Western Art: A Sampling

Peter Paul Rubens gave his sirens fishtail legs, but in other respects, including their embonpoint, *they are exactly like the opulent earthbound ladies that he painted. These are from the foreground of his splendidly flamboyant canvas* The Landing of Marie de Médicis at Marseilles, *where they all but steal the show from Marie herself.*

TEXT CONTINUED FROM PAGE 131

*Dagon his name; sea monster, upward man
And downward fish.*

The earliest female ancestor of the mermaid in human belief is probably the Semitic moon-goddess Atergatis, or Derceto. Lucian described her as having "the half of a woman, and from the thighs downwards a fish's tail." We may be surprised that a moon-goddess should have had such a decidedly fishy shape, but there is an interesting reason for this. Our ancestors observed that the moon often rose from the sea, and returned to it once more when its course over the night sky was run. It was clear that during the hours when the moon-goddess was invisible beneath the ocean she must be endowed with the power of swimming. That her shape should be partially fishlike was therefore reasonable enough.

Apart from such important deities as Oannes, Dagon, and Atergatis, the sea spawned a great host of other mermaid ancestors and relations. Typical of these were the tritons, who were not, as is generally believed, exclusively male, but included true mermaids who acted as attendants to sea divinities. Incidentally, the tritons also produced a remarkable subspecies in the creatures known as ichthyocentaurs, or centauro-tritons. These had the forefeet of a horse as well as human upper parts and a fish's tail.

Another group of mythological figures ancestral to the mermaids were the sirens. These were the offspring of the river-god Achelous and one of those attractive nymphs who seem to have been so readily available to the more influential gods in Greek mythology. They were represented in earlier art by birds with the heads of women, and later by women with the legs of birds. They are never correctly shown with a fishlike tail, this not having been one of their aids to allure, but they greatly influenced the mermaid legend by their character. The sirens were regarded as the very acme of marine sex appeal, luring mariners to destruction by seductive movements and beguiling songs (page 130) quite as effectively as the modern bikini girl ensnares incautious millionaires with a sinuous walk and a repertoire of husky contralto compliments. The treacherous beauty of the sirens was later transferred to the true mermaids, who were alleged to be irresistible to any male lucky enough to observe one.

As classical science evolved, doubts began to arise as to whether tritons, sirens, and mermaids were real or imaginary creatures. Myth and legend played such an important part in classical life that they often became confused with reality, and to the ordinary person the existence of mermaids would have been as indisputable as the existence of cod. But following on the more scientific approach to natural history which originated with the work of Aristotle a greater degree of scepticism began to prevail. Learned men demanded a more palpable proof of the existence and nature of living things than could be provided by oral tradition and unsupported travelers' tales. Nevertheless, the magical element in natural science persisted, and even Pliny, the matter-of-fact cavalry officer who wrote the second great work of natural science in the history of the world, defended the existence of mermaids with a gallantry worthy of his profession and rank. In the words of his seventeenth-century English translator, Philemon Holland, he writes: "And as far as the Meremaids, it is no fabulous tale that goeth of them: for looke how painters draw them, so they are indeed: only their bodie is rough and skaled all over, even in those parts where they resemble a woman. For such a meremaid was seene and beheld plainely upon a coast neere to the shore: and the inhabitants dwelling neer, heard it a farre off when it was a dying, to make pitteous mone, crying and chattering very heavily."

The belief that mermaids were real creatures persisted, as we have seen, throughout the Middle Ages and Renaissance, and in some quarters into the period of living memory. In the nineteenth century it was reinforced by the appearance in Europe and America of a number of stuffed mermaids which were put on exhibition by enterprising showmen. These, it was claimed, had been caught in eastern waters by intrepid fishermen, and must be regarded as final and unquestionable proof of the mermaid's real existence. Many, indeed, accepted the stuffed mermaids as the last word on the subject, and quite rejected the statements of experts who said that these creatures were concocted from the rear of a fish and the upper part of a monkey cleverly sewn together at the waist.

Now what has modern science to say concerning the mermaid legend? Zoologists of the best sort are not usually of an unromantic disposition, but the disciplines of

THE

Wonder of Wonders

BEING

A Strange and Wonderful Relation of a Mermaid, that was seen and spoke with, on the Black Rock nigh Liverpool, by John Robinson Mariner, who was tossed on the Ocean for Six days and Nights; Together with the Conversation he had with her and how he was preserved; with the Manner of his Death five days after his return Home.

LICENSED AND ENTERED ACCORDING TO ORDER.

This title page graced a 19th-century account of a meeting with a mermaid, who is characteristically shown combing her hair.

their science cannot unfortunately be stretched quite far enough to admit the existence of real mermaids. It is obvious, they say, that the numerous observations made during the history of the legend must be based on cases of mistaken identity. If this is so, what animals of the sea are most likely to have caused the error?

Two groups of animals are usually favored for this romantic role: the seals of the family *Phocidae* and the order of *Sirenia*, or sirens, known to the less poetic naturalists as sea cows. It is certainly possible that seals have been responsible for many of the mermaid reports originating in northern and temperate waters, including the glamourous vision vouchsafed to Mr. William Munro off the coast of Caithness. Those who have only observed seals as captives in the zoo will have little idea how mermaidlike they can look when seen from a cliff top in the wild. Their bodies taper to a point, resembling the typical mermaid tail, their handlike foreflippers have a most human character, and their plump, expressive faces and soft intelligent eyes are considerably more attractive than those of most of the human females available to mariners in British ports. Moreover, they have a habit of lying in languid attitudes on rocks, or poising themselves in the water when swimming so that only the forepart of their bodies protrude above the surface. Many naturalists have commented on their human appearance when in such poses, and it is easy to see how a glimpse of a seal at dusk or in a stormy sea could lead an untrained observer to suppose he had seen a mermaid.

The mermaid sightings in tropical waters are more likely to have been accounted for by a member of the order of sea cows. This name (admittedly a most unfortunate one in the present context) is borne by only three familiar species, two living and one extinct. The extinct species, known as *Rhytina stelleri*, or Steller's sea cow, was killed off only a little over a hundred years ago, and could thus have played a part in the mermaid legend (illustration at right). But as it grew regularly to between twenty and thirty feet long, and few observers have described mermaids quite as robust as this, the honor is better left to the two smaller living sea cows, known respectively as the manatee and the dugong.

Both these creatures inhabit tropic coasts. The manatee lives in the rivers and estuaries of eastern America and western Africa; the dugong in the Indian Ocean and along the shores of Australia and the East Indies. The resemblance of these animals to mermaids is based on their general anatomical shape rather than any special pretensions to glamour. Their bodies are about the same size as a woman's, they have handlike forelimbs, and their ample, rounded breasts are in the human position on the upper part of the trunk. There are no hind limbs at all, and the body tapers to a horizontally flattened tail. In other respects they have few charms except great mildness of temperament. They have a thick, cleft upper lip, and a somewhat vacant expression; the dugong's face is decidedly whiskered. Yet these characteristics are only apparent to close inspection, and it is by no means unlikely that some of the mermaid reports from Africa and Asia have been inspired by a distant or indistinct view of a sea cow in the act of submerging.

There we can say that the natural history of the mermaid is at an end. In spite of the belated intrusion of seals and sea cows into the picture, the story is not without romance. It began in the questing spirits of our ancestors, who conjured from the chaos of the waters a vision of a god symbolizing the majesty of the sea and the wonder that lies at the heart of the natural world. From these cosmic beginnings the hunger for glamour in the souls of men produced a vision at once more human and more alluring, more sensual and more dangerous—a vision of beauty in the form of a woman with a fish's tail. This infinitely desirable being manifested herself in many guises according to the age and region in which she was conceived—as Atergatis, the goddess of the moon, as the sirens, beckoning Ulysses and his heroic companions to destruction on a rocky island of the western sea, and as the mermaid herself, a haunting and mysterious symbol of human desire. If at last we find that the familiar seal and the stolid sea cow have played a part in creating this symbol, we need not be unduly depressed, for these animals too are part of the universal wonder in the world. They share with the mermaid a secure place in man's impassioned vision of the universe.

Richard Carrington is a fellow of the Royal Anthropological Institute and the Royal Geographical Society, author of Mermaids and Mastodons, *and a writer for the BBC.*

VALENTIJN, *Natural History of Amboina* 1726

CULVER SERVICE

Top: Steller's sea cow, now extinct, is sometimes suggested as the original mermaid, but its unromantic bulk (3½ tons) makes it a dismaying candidate. Middle: Valentijn's petite Amboina mermaid, or "Zee-Wyf," was "in proportion as an eel" and wore a tutu of seaweed. Bottom: In 1860 Harper's Weekly *published this engraving of "the real Japanese mermaid" accompanied by a testimonial from one Dr. D. B. Phillips of the United States Navy: "I have examined it with the utmost care, and am fully persuaded that it is genuine." Others were persuaded that it was a monkey stitched to a fish.*

OVERLEAF: *A* Buch der Natur *published in Augsburg, 1475, shows two mermaids among other odd specimens of "nature."*

135